Fast,
Fresh,
and
Spicy
Vegetarian

Fast, Fresh, and Spicy Vegetarian

Healthful Eating for the Cook on the Run

John Ettinger

PRIMA PUBLISHING

P Prima™ is a trademark of Prima Publishing, a division of Prima Communications, Inc.
Prima Publishing™ is a trademark of Prima Communications, Inc.

Tabasco® is a trademark of the McIlhenny Co.

Library of Congress Cataloging-in-Publication Data
Ettinger, John.
    Fast, fresh, and spicy vegetarian : healthful eating for the cook on the run / John Ettinger.
    p. cm.
    Includes index.
    ISBN 1-55958-694-X
    1. Vegetarian cookery. 2. Spices. I. Title.
TX837.E88   1995
641.5'636—dc20   94-39023
                                         CIP

96 97 AA 10 9 8 7 6 5 4 3 2

Printed in the United States of America

About the Nutritional Information
A per serving nutritional breakdown is provided for each recipe in this book. If a range is given for the amount of an ingredient, the breakdown is based on an average of the figures given. Also, figures are rounded up or down. Nutritional content may vary depending on the specific brands or types of ingredients used. "Optional" ingredients or those for which no specific amount is stated are not included in the breakdown.

Contents

Introduction   1
   How to Use Fresh Herbs   7
   Pepper Chart   8

1. Sauces, Salsas, and Dressings   9
   Jalapeño and Lime Dressing   11
   Cucumber-Dill Dressing   12
   Cumin and Dill Dressing   12
   Hot Vinegar   14
   Greek Dressing   14
   Three Fresh Dressings   16
   Harissa   18
   Black Bean Salsa   18
   Spicy Avocado Salsa   20
   Spicy Peach Salsa   21
   Pineapple Salsa   22
   Pizza Sauce   23
   Hot Pesto   24
   Spicy Enchilada Sauce   24
   Mexican Green Sauce   26

2. Salads   27
   Spicy Vegetable Salad   29
   Spicy Black Bean and Pasta Salad   30
   Curried Waldorf Salad   32
   Sweet Spinach Salad   33
   Sweet & Spicy Slaw   34
   Black Bean and Pepper Salad   35
   Vegetable Salad   36
   Warm Pasta Salad   37
   Thai Noodle Salad   38
   Watercress, Gorgonzola, and Pear Salad   40
   Thai Cucumber Salad   42

Curried Apple Coleslaw   43
Potato-Jicama Salad   44
Green Bean Salad   46
Jicama Slaw with Cilantro Vinaigrette   47
Colorful Rice and Black Bean Salad   48
Black Bean Vegetable Salad   50
Cucumber and Dill Salad   51
Ziti Vegetable Salad   52
Spicy Corn Salad   53
Spicy Pasta and Chickpea Salad   54
Bean Salsa with Orange Vinaigrette   56

3. Soups & Stews   57

Vegetable Broth   58
Pepperpot Soup   60
Dilled Zucchini Soup   62
Curried Vegetable Soup   63
Thai Soup   64
Curried Corn Soup   66
Cabbage Soup   67
Zucchini-Basil Soup   68
Quick Vegetable Stew   70
Red Pepper Soup   71
Spicy Corn Chowder   72
Spicy Tomato Soup   74
Gazapacho & Creamy Gazapacho   75
Cold Tomato and Roasted Pepper Soup   76
Tomato, Pepper, and Cilantro Soup   77
Cold, Spicy Cucumber Soup   78
Avocado Soup   79

4. Companion Dishes   81

Stir-Fried Red Potatoes   82
Asparagus with Ginger-Lemon Dressing   83
Hot, Spicy Rice and Raisins   84
Simple Summer Vegetables   86
Tomatoes with Parsley   87
Gruyère Potatoes   88

Quick Mexican Vegetables   89
Spicy Greens and Beans   90
Spicy Green Beans   91
Rice with Cheese   92
Sweet & Hot Carrots   93
Snappy Garbanzos   94
Mediterranean Rice   95
Gingered Black Beans   96
Simple & Spicy Zucchini Fritters   97
Spanish Rice   98
Carrot and Cilantro Rice   99
Teriyaki Mushrooms and Peppers   100
Lemon Herb Rice   101
Spicy Potato Pancakes   102
Saucy Carrots and Green Beans   103
Green Beans in Hazelnut Butter   104
Pineapple-Curry Rice   105
Raw Vegetables with Soy-Ginger Sauce   106
Curried Fried Rice   107

5. Pasta and Pizza   109

Lime-Curry Orzo   111
Lemon Spaghetti   112
Penne with Calamata Olives   113
Ratatouille Pizza   114
Penne with Peppers   116
Fettuccine with Garlic and Zucchini   117
Fettuccine with Peas and Peppers   118
Spaghetti Verdura   119
Peppers Stuffed with Pasta and Cheese   120
Mushroom-Ginger Pasta   122
Sicilian Pizza   123
Spaghetti with Hot Pepper Sauce   124
Penne with Broccoli   125
Ziti with Herbs   126
Fresh Tomato Fettuccine   128
Asian "Pesto" Pasta   129

6. Main Dishes 131

Vegetable Stir-Fry with Ginger Sauce 132
Chile and Sour Cream Quesadillas 134
Sweet & Sour & Spicy 136
Vegetarian Burritos 138
Three-Pepper Chili 140
Spicy Shish Kabobs 142
Mushroom and Cilantro Tostadas 144
Mexican Stuffed Peppers 146
Fiery Zucchini Casserole 148
Vegetable-Pepper Casserole 149
Black Bean One-Skillet Casserole 150
Mex-Italian Frittata 151
Colorful Couscous Casserole 152
Andrew's Mushroom Ta-Rito 154
Hot & Spicy Fried Rice 155
Mexican "Quiche" 156
Curried Vegetables 158
Pepper and Bean Enchiladas with Green Sauce 160
Grilled Vegetables with Ginger Barbecue Sauce 162
Zucchini Stuffed with Herbs and Cheese 164
Cheese, Tomato, and Hot Pepper Sandwiches 166
Spicy Eggplant Casserole 167
Four-Alarm Stir-Fry 168
Black Bean and Jicama Tostadas 170
Potatoes and Rice with Spice 171
Fruit Curry over Rice 172
Baked Zucchini with Pepper Sauce 174
Vegetables in Raw Tomato Sauce 176
Pineapple Stir-Fried Rice 178
Sweet & Sour Cabbage 179
Vegetables in Spanish Rice 180

Index 183
International Conversion Chart 198

Acknowledgments

Thank you to Andi Reese Brady, Marianne Rogoff, and the staff at Prima for their help, and especially to Jennifer Basye Sander for her enthusiasm and encouragement. I couldn't continue doing these books without friends like Velma Tepper, Penny Kozar, Virginia Phillips, John Lien, Steve and Sarah Cooper, Becky Maloney, Brenda Lawrence, Carol Strauch, and Mary Fryday. Thanks especially to steadfast tester and questioner Connie Elaine.

Introduction

There is no tofu in this book. For those who think vegetarian is tofu and sprouts, welcome to the '90s, where vegetarian is peppers and pasta, curries and cold soups.

I confess to not being vegetarian. However, like so many others, we eat less meat, less fat, and more healthful foods. I cook almost everything from scratch—not because I'm overly ambitious but because my son Joseph, who is eight, has food allergies, so we forego the luxury of convenience foods or restaurant meals. This means no pizza (dairy) or other fast foods, no convenience foods (soy and corn)—not even candy (corn syrup). Before you feel sorry for him, look at the color in his cheeks and the sparkle of his blue eyes and feel the energy of a little boy who eats few artificial ingredients, little fat, and literally bushels of fruit. If one apple a day truly keeps the doctor away, he is covered for thirty years or so. His diet has us all eating less fat and much more healthful foods than we did before he came into our lives.

I grew up on the straight-ahead food of the '50s and '60s, but the food had flavor. I remember my mother, all of 5'1", standing on her toes and peering into her spice rack to make selections for "a little of this and a little of that," which were the standard ingredients in her recipes, or at least that's what she'd tell you. I've never been sure whether she doesn't remember or doesn't care to tell.

We've come a long way from the heavy foods of that era. Now we want foods that are fast, fresh, and full of flavor. Toward that end, here are some thoughts on using ingredients to get the most out of this book.

Oils   When specified, use extra-virgin olive oil. I always use this premium oil when making dressings or in any dish where the flavor of the oil is important. Extra-virgin olive oil has less than 1 percent acidity and comes from the first press of the olives. Cold-press means the olives were crushed with granite stones (the only stone that will retain cold). Pure olive oil is made from a second or third pressing. For most sautéing or cooking, you can use a less expensive olive oil.

Buy your olive oil in a can if you don't use a great deal. Light and warmth can cause olive oil to spoil more quickly, so it's a good idea to store olive oils in a cool, dark place.

For other vegetable oils I use canola or sunflower oil, but often olive oil will do as well.

Vinegars   Common wine vinegars—wine, cider, rice, and balsamic—are used throughout this book for dressings and sauces. Red wine vinegar is best suited for sauces and marinades, white vinegar for herb dressings and emulsions, rice vinegar for oriental cuisine, and balsamic vinegar for sauces and dressings. A good-quality vinegar will give your foods more depth (quality is especially important with balsamic vinegar, which should be from Modena).

Herbs and Spices   A few dishes in the book call specifically for fresh ingredients, and there is no substituting dried. For example, if you substitute dried ginger for fresh, grated ginger, it will completely change the flavor of the dish. The same is true for fresh or dried cilantro (also known as coriander). There is simply no comparison. The taste of tarragon and rosemary may be lost if you substitute dried for fresh, although the difference isn't too great for making sauces.

Some herbs have such a delicate taste that they should only be added at the end of a dish, just before serving. Chervil, parsley, chives, salad burnet, summer savory, watercress, and marjoram generally suffer over high heat.

You can increase the life of fresh herbs by storing them in the refrigerator with the stems in water or wrapped with a damp paper towel, the tops covered with a plastic bag. The chart on page 7 is a general guide for matching herbs to the type of dish you are preparing.

Finding fresh garlic can sometimes be a problem. Supermarkets routinely sell garlic that has been on the shelf too long. Looks for heads with tight, papery skin and firm cloves, be they purple or white. Spring is the best time to find great garlic.

Peppers Most hot peppers can be exchanged for others in recipes, so don't be disappointed if jalapeños are the only pepper you can find (see Pepper Chart on page 8). If you are using a pepper that is hotter than the recommended one, simply use less. Whether you like your dishes hotter or milder, choose a pepper to match your taste.

Be **cautious** cooking with hot peppers. A little pepper on the finger, inadvertently rubbed into the eye (even if it happens a little later), is extremely painful and dangerous. Use gloves or wash up well after using peppers, especially the extremely hot varieties.

Beans I'm pretty satisfied most of the time using canned beans, especially black beans. If you want to use dried, soak them overnight in cold water after first picking out any stones. To quick-soak beans, cover them with water and bring to a boil.

Boil, covered, for a couple of minutes, remove from heat, and let sit for at least an hour. Drain and use fresh water for cooking.

Peeling and Roasting A few of the recipes call for peeled tomatoes or roasted peppers. To peel and seed tomatoes, drop them into boiling water for about 15 seconds. Drain and peel them. Then cut the tomatoes in half crosswise and gently squeeze out the seeds.

To roast hot or sweet peppers, first char them under a broiler, turning frequently, until blackened. Put them in a paper bag, close tightly, and let steam for 20 minutes or so. The skin should come off quickly and easily. Jars of roasted peppers are also available in many grocery stores.

Chili and Curry Powder A friend tried a recipe of mine once and I could tell from her expression that she didn't like it. It turned out she had used a store-brand chili powder in a dish where the quality of the chili powder meant everything. Once I supplied her with good powder her opinion of the recipe changed dramatically.

There are inferior chili and curry powders on the market, and since quality can make all the difference in some dishes, it is worth it to pay a little extra for spice which will flavor your dish properly. Especially watch out for store brands. If you have time, stop by a cookware or health food store and get a good-quality powder.

Other Ingredients Yogurt used in these recipes is plain, non-fat or lowfat. The nutritional analysis is based on using nonfat yogurt. Kosher salt is recommended for my recipes since it has less bite than iodized salt.

Fast, Fresh, and Spicy Vegetarian is about cooking for today's lifestyles. We all know the importance of "fast" in our lives, and "spicy" is a goal for an increasing number of cooks. The third element, "fresh," speaks to our wish for good health since fresh foods are without a doubt richer in vitamins and minerals.

In the media blitz over "The French Paradox" the past couple of years, the tendency to use fresh ingredients in France has been downplayed or ignored. You may recall that it was reported in studies that the French have fewer heart problems than Americans despite a diet rich in butter and cream. The reports suggested that it may be because wine plays such a big part in the diet, since the French consume wine with most lunches and dinners. The connection is certainly valid, since so many others have reported the health value of a little wine.

Equally valid, yet given scant attention, is how likely the French are to use fresh ingredients. While Americans gulp record liters of soda pop and are hooked on processed foods, the French will generally eat fresh foods rather than microwave a dinner from the freezer.

Fresh foods *are* healthier. It's also true that choosing produce wisely is hard. Your best bet is to celebrate the best that is available for the current season. By using what is in season you are most likely to be happy with what you create.

Finally, ignore those voices who say that vegetarians are missing something. What vegetarians miss most is the high cholesterol and saturated fat of many animal products. And of course, grains, beans, fruits, and vegetables are easier to digest than meat. Vegetarians have markedly lower rates of certain diseases, including heart disease and colon cancer. The myth of a protein deficiency is simply that—a myth. Any vegetarian concerned about protein can throw a handful of roasted nuts onto a salad or add some canned beans (more protein per dollar than any other food, but without the fat and cholesterol) to a soup. Protein is available from beans and nuts, and also from bread, rice, corn, cottage cheese, eggs, milk, pasta, potatoes, split peas, and yogurt.

Vegetables are rich in vitamins. Sweet potatoes, tomatoes, and Brussels sprouts contain vitamin C; in fact, a sweet pepper has twice as much vitamin C as an orange. For calcium, try parsley and leaf lettuce; for iron, eat peas, raisins, or spinach; to get more vitamin A, enjoy carrots, broccoli, cantaloupe, or sweet red peppers. Only vitamin B12 is difficult to gain through vegetarian cooking but it needn't be, thanks to so many grains and cereals fortified with this vitamin.

Those who talk about deficiencies for vegetarians never seem to mention the many deficiencies inherent in the meaty diets of most Americans. Vegetarian eating is good for your health.

I had a wonderful time creating these recipes. I hope you enjoy them.

How to Use Fresh Herbs

Add this herb to . . .	Salads	Dressings	Sauces	Soups	Stews	
Basil	Yes	No	Yes	Yes	No	Add to soups just before done.
Bay Leaf	No	No	Yes	Yes	Yes	Especially good in any tomato-based sauce.
Chervil	Yes	Yes	Yes	Yes	Yes	Versatile, anise-like, best in salads and soups.
Chives	Yes	Yes	Yes	No	No	A delicate onion flavor.
Cilantro	Yes	Yes	Yes	Yes	No	Be sure the flavor of cilantro complements the other ingredients.
Dill Weed	Yes	Yes	Yes	Yes	No	Gives a sweet flavor; goes well with thyme.
Garlic	No	Yes	Yes	Yes	Yes	Almost a must with oil & vinegar dressing.
Marjoram	No	Yes	Yes	Yes	Yes	Try it fresh in scrambled eggs.
Mint Leaves	Yes	Yes	Yes	No	No	Surprise flavor in salads and dressings.
Oregano	No	Yes	Yes	Yes	Yes	With oil & vinegar it makes a Greek salad.
Parsley	Yes	Yes	Yes	Yes	Yes	Use more if using milder flat-leaf.
Rosemary	No	Yes	Yes	Yes	Yes	Has the power to refresh foods—and you.
Sage	No	No	Yes	No	Yes	Strong flavor, use sparingly.
Summer Savory	Yes	Yes	Yes	Yes	Yes	Thyme-like but more peppery.
Tarragon	No	Yes	Yes	Yes	Yes	Subtle flavor goes a long way.
Thyme	No	Yes	Yes	Yes	Yes	Staple for fresh vegetables.
Watercress	Yes	Yes	Yes	No	No	Peppery, pungent, and very perishable.

Pepper Chart

Pepper Name	Heat (0 = mild; 10 = hot)	Uses/Colors
Ancho AKA: Pablano (fresh)	3 to 6	Dried pepper is dark brown. Use in sauces.

Banana
  AKA: Hungarian Yellow
    Wax and Sweet Banana
	0 to 3	Yellow-green, yellow and red. Use fresh, not dried, in salads, vegetable dishes, stews.

Bell AKA: Capsicums	0	Green, red, purple, yellow, orange. All are sweet. Use stuffed, in salads, sauces, relishes, casseroles, sautéed.
Cayenne	7	Most commonly powdered spice. Use in Indian and Cajun recipes, and dressings. Fresh are red to dark green.
Cherry	0 to 4	Usually added to condiments and relishes.
Chipotle	5	Dried, green to red. Use in sauces and seasonings.
de Arbol	8	Green or red. Almost always used dried.
Fresno AKA: Hot chile pepper	6 to 7	Use fresh only as a seasoning. Yellow-green, occasionally red.
Guajillo	5	Green or red. Use in sauces or seasonings.
Habanero	10	Green, orange. Extremely hot. Use in cooked sauces, pastes.
Italian AKA: Cubanelle	0	Red or green. Stuff or use as a substitute for bell peppers.
Jalapeño AKA: Bola	5 to 7	Black-green to red. Use in stews, soups, sauces, salsas, and pastes.
New Mexican AKA: Anaheim	1 to 3	Green to red. Use in soups, stews, sauces, and stuffed.
Pasilla AKA: Chilaca (fresh)	4	Brown to black. Primarily used in sauces.
Scotch bonnet	10	Green to orange. Extremely hot. Use in sauces.
Serrano	7 to 8	Green to red. Used in many sauces.
Tabasco	9	Very hot. Use as a seasoning.
Tomato	0 to 2	Sweet, red or green. Source for paprika.

1

Sauces, Salsas, and Dressings

I am puzzled when I see the vast array of bottled dressings in supermarkets. Why pay so much for something that costs so little to make, takes so little time, and tastes so much better when fresh? Homemade dressings taste so good that it will be hard to go back to bottled once you learn how easy it is to make your own.

Dressings are simply a mixture of fat and acid, usually oil and vinegar, mixed at 2:1 or 3:1. There are two basic types of dressings. The first are the vinaigrettes, a combination of fat and acid blended with herbs, spices, and other enhancements. The second type uses an emulsifier to stabilize the suspension of the fat and acid, ranging from an egg yolk or yogurt in creamy dressings to basil in pesto. Oil, vinegar, and flavor: so simple and quick.

Mixing in herbs and spices is easy enough, and you can always substitute mild herbs to make use of what's on hand, or to create something different for your family or guests. One thing is certain: once you understand how easy it is to make your own dressings, how much more flavorful they are, and how much less they cost, you won't spend much time in that dressing aisle.

Salsas can also be made quickly. Homemade salsas give the cook the advantage of making them to match the dish. Bean salsas are very quick, while tomato salsas take a little longer, and really need fresh tomatoes to be at their best. A salsa is just a mixture of fresh ingredients and, when it comes to salsas, black beans are a cook's best friend. (I think black beans are a cook's best friend, period. Always keep a can on hand and you will be able to make a quick, last-minute meal or late night-snack.)

Sauces can be the busy and creative cook's salvation. Sauces can turn the everyday into something different and exciting. Curries can be added to rice, pepper sauces to tortillas, and olive oil sauces to pasta. Dressings, salsas, and sauces are included in other recipes in the book, but here are a few favorites I didn't want to leave out.

Jalapeño and Lime Dressing

Pour this dressing over vegetables, sliced jicama, or sweet peppers. It's especially good with Mexican foods.

2 teaspoons jalapeño, seeded and minced
1/4 cup fresh lime juice
2 tablespoons vegetable oil
1/4 teaspoon salt
Pinch of oregano

Mix all ingredients together.

Makes 1/2 cup

Each 2 tablespoon serving provides:

65	Calories	2 g	Carbohydrate
0 g	Protein	133 mg	Sodium
7 g	Fat	0 mg	Cholesterol

Cucumber-Dill Dressing

PREPARATION TIME: 10 minutes

This is good over greens and mild vegetables such as zucchini.

1	cucumber, peeled, seeded, and chopped
1/4	cup fresh dill, chopped
1	cup sour cream
2	tablespoons vinegar

Place all ingredients in a blender and process until smooth.

Makes 3 cups

Each 2 tablespoon serving provides:

19	Calories	1 g	Carbohydrate
0 g	Protein	5 mg	Sodium
2 g	Fat	3 mg	Cholesterol

Cumin and Dill Dressing

PREPARATION TIME: 5 minutes

Another good dressing for greens. When you are preparing Mexican food, add a few greens to the plate and top with this quick dressing.

3	tablespoons extra-virgin olive oil
1	tablespoon lime vinegar
1	teaspoon dried dill
1/4	teaspoon cumin
1/8	teaspoon salt

Mix all ingredients together.

Makes 1/4 cup

Each 2 tablespoon serving provides:

182	Calories	1 g	Carbohydrate
0 g	Protein	135 mg	Sodium
20 g	Fat	0 mg	Cholesterol

Hot Vinegar

PREPARATION TIME: 5 minutes (plus 30 minutes or more
marinating time)

*Use this simple vinegar to put a little fire into soups, or use it in
a vinaigrette.*

6   tablespoons white vinegar
1/4   teaspoon salt
1   hot chile pepper (see Pepper Chart on page 8 to choose
        the heat level you want), seeded and cut into thin slices

Mix all ingredients and let sit for 30 minutes or longer. Discard
the pepper. (Keeps about a week in the refrigerator.)

Makes 6 tablespoons

Each 1 tablespoon serving provides:

2	Calories	1 g	Carbohydrate
0 g	Protein	89 mg	Sodium
0 g	Fat	0 mg	Cholesterol

Greek Dressing

PREPARATION TIME: 5 minutes

*A Greek-style salad is such a nice and colorful accompaniment
to so many dishes, I've included this simple standard. Toss*

dressing with chopped, fresh vegetables, such as tomato, sweet pepper, and onion, or with almost any vegetable salad. Don't forget the feta cheese.

$1/2$ cup extra-virgin olive oil
$1/4$ cup red wine vingar
$1/2$ teaspoon fresh lemon juice
$1 1/2$ teaspoons fresh oregano or $1/2$ teaspoon dried
$1/4$ teaspoon salt
$1/4$ teaspoon pepper

Whisk all together.

Makes $3/4$ cup

Each 2 tablespoon serving provides:

160	Calories	1 g	Carbohydrate
0 g	Protein	89 mg	Sodium
18 g	Fat	0 mg	Cholesterol

Three Fresh Dressings

Use these quick dressings for greens or vegetable salads. Or use vinaigrette for Yukon Gold or other small potatoes which have been cooked, sliced, and cooled.

Rosemary Vinaigrette

$1/2$	cup extra-virgin olive oil
$1/4$	cup balsamic vinegar
3	tablespoons lemon juice
1	clove garlic, minced
$1/2$	teaspoon fresh rosemary, chopped
$1/8$	teaspoon salt
$1/8$	teaspoon pepper

Whisk all together.

Makes 1 cup

Each 2 tablespoon serving provides:

129	Calories	2 g	Carbohydrate
0 g	Protein	35 mg	Sodium
14 g	Fat	0 mg	Cholesterol

Honey Mustard Dressing

1	tablespoon honey
1	tablespoon Dijon mustard
1/2	cup extra-virgin olive oil
2	tablespoons white wine vinegar
1/4	teaspoon salt
1/2	teaspoon pepper

Whisk all together.

Makes 2/3 cup

Each 2 tablespoon serving provides:

174	Calories	4 g	Carbohydrate
0 g	Protein	157 mg	Sodium
18 g	Fat	0 mg	Cholesterol

Wine Vinaigrette

1/4	cup white wine vinegar
1/4	cup dry white wine
1/3	cup peanut oil
1/3	cup extra-virgin olive oil
1	clove garlic, minced

Whisk all together.

Makes 1 1/4 cups

Each 2 tablespoon serving provides:

131	Calories	1 g	Carbohydrate
0 g	Protein	1 mg	Sodium
14 g	Fat	0 mg	Cholesterol

Harissa

PREPARATION TIME: 10 minutes

This very hot sauce is from Morocco, where it is used to spice up couscous. Try a little with rice dishes.

8	hot peppers (1/3 to 1/2 cup), stemmed, seeded, and chopped
1	teaspoon caraway seeds
4	cloves garlic, peeled
1/3	cup olive oil
	Salt

Put all ingredients in a blender and puree.

Makes about 3/4 cup

Each 1 tablespoon serving provides:

57	Calories	1 g	Carbohydrate
0 g	Protein	1 mg	Sodium
6 g	Fat	0 mg	Cholesterol

Black Bean Salsa

PREPARATION TIME: 25 minutes (plus 30 minutes standing time)

A staple in my kitchen, black bean salsa in a tortilla is a meal unto itself. Or serve it alongside any Mexican foods. (If you are in a hurry, it works fine with fresh, non-roasted peppers.)

2	cups black beans, canned okay (see Introduction, page 3)
1/4	to 1/2 jalapeño, roasted, peeled, and seeded
	Juice of 1 lime
1/2	cup jicama, chopped
1 1/2	tablespoons fresh cilantro, chopped
1/2	red or white onion, finely chopped
1/8	teaspoon cumin
1/8	teaspoon salt
1/4	teaspoon pepper
1	teaspoon fresh ginger, grated (optional)

Mix all ingredients and let sit 30 minutes.

Makes 3 1/2 cups

Each 1/4 cup serving provides:

36	Calories	7 g	Carbohydrate
2 g	Protein	148 mg	Sodium
0 g	Fat	0 mg	Cholesterol

Spicy Avocado Salsa

PREPARATION TIME: 15 minutes

Wonderful with Mexican foods, and easy to make with no need to peel tomatoes or roast peppers.

2   avocados, diced
2   tomatoes, diced
2   serrano, seeded and minced
1/2   cup extra-virgin olive oil
      Juice of 2 limes
3   tablespoons fresh cilantro, chopped
1/4   teaspoon ground cumin
1/8   teaspoon salt

Combine all ingredients.

Makes 4 cups

Each 1/4 cup serving provides:

106	Calories	3 g	Carbohydrate
1 g	Protein	22 mg	Sodium
11 g	Fat	0 mg	Cholesterol

Spicy Peach Salsa

PREPARATION TIME: 15 minutes

Fruit salsas are popular in the Caribbean where they are served with many fish dishes. Try this with rice or curries.

3   large, firm, ripe peaches, diced
1   red bell pepper, seeded and finely chopped
1   sweet onion, cut in half and thinly sliced
3   tablespoons fresh cilantro, chopped
3   tablespoons fresh parsley, chopped
1/2   teaspoon jalapeño, seeded and minced
1   tablespoon honey
1   clove garlic, minced
       Juice of 3 limes
1/4   cup extra-virgin olive oil

Mix all ingredients well.

Makes 5 1/2 cups

~~~~~~~~~~~~

Each 1/4 cup serving provides:

36	Calories	4 g	Carbohydrate
0 g	Protein	1 mg	Sodium
3 g	Fat	0 mg	Cholesterol

Pineapple Salsa

Preparation Time: 15 minutes

This salsa is delicious alongside many rice dishes or simply for dipping.

2	cups pineapple, cut into rings
1/2	red bell pepper, seeded and diced
1/2	green bell pepper, seeded and diced
1/2	red onion, finely chopped
1/4	cup vegetable oil
2	tablespoons fresh cilantro, chopped
1	tablespoon lime juice
1	tablespoon fresh parsley, chopped
1	teaspoon red pepper flakes

Place pineapple on a lightly oiled baking sheet. Broil each side until brown, about 5 minutes each. Remove from oven and cool. Dice pineapple and mix with remaining ingredients.

Makes 4 cups

Each 1/4 cup serving provides:

57	Calories	7 g	Carbohydrate
0 g	Protein	1 mg	Sodium
4 g	Fat	0 mg	Cholesterol

Pizza Sauce

PREPARATION TIME: 30 minutes

With the new focaccia and ready-to-bake pizza breads—not to mention bread machines—good bread for pizza is readily available. However, the quality of bottled and even refrigerated sauces hasn't kept up.

This quick sauce, combined with your choice of vegetables and some oregano sprinkled on top, can mean terrific homemade pizza in minutes. The sauce will keep in the freezer for 6 weeks or so, or in the refrigerator for a couple of days.

1/4	cup extra-virgin olive oil
1	small onion, finely chopped
4	cloves garlic, minced
1	28-ounce can crushed tomatoes in juice
1	tablespoon dried dill
1	tablespoon dried thyme
2	bay leaves

Place the oil, onion, and garlic in an unheated saucepan and stir to coat. Cook over moderate-low heat until garlic just begins to turn golden (but do not brown), 3 to 4 minutes. Add the tomatoes and seasonings, bring to a boil, reduce heat and simmer for 20 minutes. Discard bay leaves.

Makes 4 cups

Each 1/4 cup serving provides:

44	Calories	3 g	Carbohydrate
0 g	Protein	83 mg	Sodium
4 g	Fat	0 mg	Cholesterol

Hot Pesto

Pesto is the easiest and one of the healthiest dishes to make—which explains its popularity. Here the pesto is spiced up with hot peppers, so you might want a cool salad on the side.

2   cups packed fresh basil leaves
3   cloves garlic, minced
1/4   cup pine nuts or sunflower seeds
1/2   jalapeño or 1 serrano, seeded and minced
1/2   cup fresh Parmesan, grated
1   cup olive oil

Place all ingredients except the oil in a blender or food processor. Add the oil slowly and puree. Toss with pasta of your choice, pour over sautéed vegetables, or add to soup.

Makes 2 cups

Each 1/4 cup serving provides:

291	Calories	2 g	Carbohydrate
4 g	Protein	94 mg	Sodium
31 g	Fat	4 mg	Cholesterol

Spicy Enchilada Sauce

PREPARATION TIME: 35 minutes (plus 1 hour soaking and 30 minutes cooking time)

This wonderful sauce, using dried peppers, keeps in the refrigerator for a week. We use it over tortillas and cheese for lunch and dinner. For quick enchiladas, simply dip warmed tortillas in the sauce and fill with cheese, onions, and chopped chiles. Roll them up, cover with more sauce, and bake until hot and bubbly. You'll find dried chiles in the Mexican food section of many supermarkets.

7	New Mexican or other dried chiles
2	cloves garlic, minced
1	onion, chopped
3	teaspoons dried oregano
1	teaspoon jalapeño, seeded and minced
1/2	teaspoon red pepper flakes
1	teaspoon ground cumin
1	cup vegetable broth or water
3	tablespoons vegetable oil
2	tablespoons flour
1	6-ounce can tomato paste

Wash the chiles and cover them with boiling water. Let stand for an hour then drain. Remove seeds and stems, and place them in a blender along with the garlic, onion, spices, jalapeño, and broth and puree.

In a skillet, heat the oil and add the flour, stirring to mix. Add the puree from the blender along with the tomato paste and a cup of water. Simmer for 30 minutes or until thickened.

Makes 4 cups

Each 1/4 cup serving provides:

66	Calories	10 g	Carbohydrate
2 g	Protein	157 mg	Sodium
3 g	Fat	0 mg	Cholesterol

Mexican Green Sauce

PREPARATION TIME: 25 minutes

This is a pretty typical Mexican green sauce—tomatillos, chiles, garlic, and onion are staples—and it does well with enchiladas or tacos. It can also be used on fritattas.

1	pound fresh tomatillos (about 11), husked and washed
2	to 3 fresh jalapeños, seeded
5	sprigs fresh cilantro, coarsely chopped
1	small onion, chopped
1	clove garlic, chopped or minced
6	to 7 fresh mint or epazote leaves (optional)
2	tablespoons vegetable oil
2	cups vegetable broth
1/4	teaspoon salt

Boil the tomatillos and jalapeños in salted water until just tender, about 10 minutes, then drain. (If using canned tomatillos, simply drain.) Place in a blender or food processor with the cilantro, onion, and garlic (and mint, if desired) and blend until smooth. Heat oil in a skillet over medium-high heat. Pour the sauce in and stir for 5 minutes. Add broth and salt, return to a boil, then simmer for 8 to 10 minutes, until thickened.

Makes 3 cups

Each 1/4 cup serving provides:

44	Calories	5 g	Carbohydrate
1 g	Protein	46 mg	Sodium
3 g	Fat	0 mg	Cholesterol

2

Salads

Salads are among the oldest recorded meals. In ancient Greece, salads were considered the foods of the gods. The Romans had exotic salads with pennyroyal (a mint), dates, truffles, and olives. They sprinkled their greens with wine.

Greeks and Romans notwithstanding, up until my twenties salads were either first courses or side dishes to pasta (nothing goes better with a hearty spaghetti sauce than a simple salad of greens with a vinaigrette).

I was twenty-something in the '70s when I moved to San Francisco and in that great city I learned that salads could be more than iceberg lettuce, supermarket tomatoes, and bottled dressing. It was there I discovered that a salad can be a great meal.

Salads of greens or beans lend themselves to the use of many spices. You might try adding a pinch of allspice or cayenne, a little mace or paprika, in dressings or atop your favorite salads. Celery, sesame, mustard, and poppy seeds are welcome additions to many salads. Tossed greens don't even have to be green anymore, with the increasing availability of radicchio and other once-exotic ingredients.

Be flexible when shopping for salad ingredients. If the ingredients you've planned on aren't that fresh, be prepared to substitute or make a salad out of what does look good. Salads, more than any other dish, are only as good as their ingredients. Select greens that are crisp and free of brown-tipped leaves. Choose cabbage and head lettuce that are heavy. If you are going to soak beans for bean salad, do so the night before, but be sure to pick out any stones. Or use the quick-soak method on page 3.

My weakness when it comes to green salads is cheese. I like to add a slice of bleu on the side or a sprinkle of Parmesan. That tendency is reflected in the Watercress, Gorgonzola, and Pear Salad (page 40).

Some of these salads are complete meals, like Spicy Black Bean and Pasta Salad (page 30), while others are best as accompaniments. As with many other recipes in this book, adjust the pepper flakes or hot peppers to suit your taste, for a hotter or milder salad.

Spicy Vegetable Salad

PREPARATION TIME: 20 minutes

The crunch of cool vegetables is offset by the spicy dressing. Good with a casserole or on its own.

2	tablespoons vegetable oil
1/2	teaspoon cumin
1/2	teaspoon dry mustard
1	teaspoon dried coriander
1	small hot pepper, seeded and minced
1/2	teaspoon fresh ginger, grated
1/3	cup yogurt
1/3	cup lowfat sour cream
2	tablespoons fresh dill
2	cucumbers, peeled, seeded, and sliced
1	sweet onion, chopped
2	tomatoes, sliced
3	carrots, thinly sliced

Stir the cumin, mustard, and coriander into oil that has been warmed over medium-low heat. Add the pepper, increase heat to medium, and stir for 1 minute. Remove from heat, add ginger, then mix with yogurt and sour cream. Stir in dill, toss well with vegetables.

Serves 4

Each 1 cup serving provides:

172	Calories	18 g	Carbohydrate
4 g	Protein	57 mg	Sodium
10 g	Fat	8 mg	Cholesterol

Spicy Black Bean and Pasta Salad

PREPARATION TIME: 20 minutes (plus 1 hour chilling time)

The very hot peppers give plenty of heat to the oil and, along with a little red pepper flakes, make this a spicy salad. Use gloves to handle the peppers—Scotch bonnet peppers are very, very hot.

1	pound thin spaghetti or vermicelli
2	tablespoons peanut oil
2	Scotch bonnet or habanero peppers, seeded, and cut into rings (use caution in handling!)
2	shallots, finely chopped
2	cloves garlic, minced
3/4	cup black beans, canned okay (see Introduction, page 3)
1/2	cup vegetable stock or water
1/8	teaspoon red pepper flakes
3	teaspoons rice vinegar

Cook pasta according to package directions. Heat oil and peppers in a small skillet until very hot, stir to blend, and remove from heat. Discard peppers and add shallots and garlic, cooking over medium-low heat for 3 to 4 minutes. Add remaining ingredients except the vinegar and cook 5 to 6 minutes longer. Remove from heat. Add vinegar, then toss with pasta, and chill 1 hour before serving.

Serves 4 as entree, 6 as side dish

Each entree serving provides:

563	Calories	101 g	Carbohydrate
19 g	Protein	181 mg	Sodium
9 g	Fat	0 mg	Cholesterol

Curried Waldorf Salad

PREPARATION TIME: 20 minutes

The original Waldorf Salad was created in New York in the late 19th century. Walnuts, now considered an integral part, were not included in the original. I've curried the idea and it makes a nice spicy salad.

2   ribs celery, sliced
3   red Delicious apples, cored and diced
1/4   cup raisins
1/4   cup scallions, chopped
1/4   cup toasted almonds, chopped
1/4   cup mayonnaise
1/4   cup plain yogurt
1   teaspoon good-quality curry powder
1/4   teaspoon fresh ginger, grated
1/8   teaspoon *each* cinnamon, allspice

Combine the celery, apples, raisins, scallions, and almonds in a bowl and toss. Mix the remaining ingredients and then toss well with the salad.

Serves 4

Each serving provides:

242	Calories	27 g	Carbohydrate
3 g	Protein	110 mg	Sodium
15 g	Fat	8 mg	Cholesterol

Sweet Spinach Salad

PREPARATION TIME: 15 minutes

Now you can get your kids to eat spinach—they'll love this sweet dressing.

1	bunch of spinach, washed and torn
1/2	red onion, cut in half and thinly sliced
4	to 5 mushrooms, sliced
3	tablespoons vegetable oil
2	tablespoons cider vinegar
2	teaspoons brown sugar

Place the spinach, onion, and mushrooms in a bowl. Whisk together the oil, vinegar, and sugar until the sugar is melted, then pour over the salad and toss.

Serves 4

Each serving provides:

129	Calories	8 g	Carbohydrate
2 g	Protein	34 mg	Sodium
11 g	Fat	0 mg	Cholesterol

Sweet & Spicy Slaw

PREPARATION TIME: 15 minutes

This is one of my favorite dishes for guests. I take it along to potlucks or serve it with a casual dinner—the color is wonderful. The gingered dressing goes well with many Asian foods.

1	small cabbage, shredded
1	red or green bell pepper, seeded and julienned
1	teaspoon serrano, seeded and finely minced
2	tablespoons vegetable oil
2	tablespoons rice vinegar
1	teaspoon brown sugar
2	teaspoons fresh ginger, grated (do not use powdered)

Toss the cabbage and peppers in a bowl. Combine the oil, vinegar, sugar, and ginger in a separate bowl. Mix well then toss with the cabbage and peppers.

Serves 6

Each serving provides:

73	Calories	8 g	Carbohydrate
1 g	Protein	19 mg	Sodium
5 g	Fat	0 mg	Cholesterol

Black Bean and Pepper Salad

PREPARATION TIME: 20 minutes

Another colorful salad that blends oil and vinegar, hot spices, and sweet peppers.

2	cups black beans, canned okay (see Introduction)
1	small sweet onion, diced
1	stalk celery, sliced
1	serrano, seeded and minced
1/2	red or green bell pepper, seeded and diced
2	tablespoons fresh cilantro, chopped
1	tablespoon lemon juice
1	clove garlic, minced
1/2	teaspoon ground cumin
1/2	teaspoon ground coriander
2	teaspoons red wine vinegar
5	tablespoons extra-virgin olive oil

Combine the beans, onion, celery, peppers, and cilantro in a bowl. In a small bowl combine the remaining ingredients then toss with the black bean mixture.

Serves 4

Each serving provides:

284	Calories	26 g	Carbohydrate
8 g	Protein	477 mg	Sodium
18 g	Fat	0 mg	Cholesterol

Vegetable Salad

PREPARATION TIME: 15 minutes (plus 1 hour chilling time)

Jicama is becoming more common in supermarkets. I enjoy the apple-like texture of this vegetable and its sweet and nutty flavor. Combined with cabbage and ginger, this salad has a hint of the Orient.

2	cups jicama, peeled and julienned into 2-inch pieces
1	cup cucumber, peeled, seeded, cut in half lengthwise, and thinly sliced
1/2	sweet onion, cut in half and thinly sliced
2	cups cabbage, shredded
2	tablespoons olive oil
1/3	cup balsamic vinegar
1	teaspoon fresh ginger, grated
1	tablespoon lemon juice

Combine the jicama, cucumber, onion, and cabbage in a bowl. Combine the remaining ingredients and pour over the vegetables. Refrigerate until chilled.

Serves 4

Each serving provides:

128	Calories	16 g	Carbohydrate
1 g	Protein	12 mg	Sodium
7 g	Fat	0 mg	Cholesterol

Warm Pasta Salad

PREPARATION TIME: 30 minutes

A great side salad or meal, especially when served with soup. For a colorful and filling meal make a two-salad plate: use this salad and Sweet Spinach Salad (page 33), or Sweet & Spicy Slaw (page 34).

12	ounces pasta shells
3	to 4 cherry tomatoes, cut in half
1/2	sweet onion, cut in half and thinly sliced
1	red or green bell pepper, seeded and thinly sliced
1/2	cup niçoise or calamata olives, pits removed and cut in half
1	tablespoon *each* lemon thyme or thyme, lemon zest, majoram, basil
2	tablespoons fresh parsley
6	tablespoons olive oil
3	tablespoons lemon juice

Cook pasta according to package directions. Meanwhile, combine the tomatoes, onion, pepper, and olives in a bowl. In a small bowl combine the remaining ingredients then toss with the vegetables. Add cooked pasta and mix well. Serve warm or at room temperature.

Serves 4

Each serving provides:

579	Calories	76 g	Carbohydrate
13 g	Protein	323 mg	Sodium
26 g	Fat	0 mg	Cholesterol

Thai Noodle Salad

PREPARATION TIME: 25 minutes (plus 30 minutes chilling time)

This cold salad is refreshing and light. Use any thin pasta or noodle you have on hand.

1	pound Asian or Italian noodles
1	small clove garlic, minced
2	tablespoons fresh lemon juice
3	tablespoons sesame or peanut oil
1/8	teaspoon hot pepper, minced (see Pepper Chart, page 8)
1/8	teaspoon red pepper flakes
1	tablespoon chives or scallions, minced
3/4	cup coconut milk
3	tablespoons fresh mint, minced
3	tablespoons fresh basil, minced
2	tablespoons fresh ginger, grated
2	carrots, sliced
1	sweet pepper, seeded and julienned
1	cup snow peas, halved
1/2	cup water chestnuts, sliced

Cook noodles according to package directions. Mix the next 10 ingredients in a bowl and set aside. Cook carrots until just tender, retaining some crispness. Blanch the pepper and snow peas, and rinse under cold water. Combine the vegetables with the water chestnuts, add the sauce, then toss with noodles. Mix well and refrigerate until cool, about 30 minutes.

Serves 4

Each serving provides:

673	Calories	102 g	Carbohydrate
18 g	Protein	31 mg	Sodium
22 g	Fat	0 mg	Cholesterol

Watercress, Gorgonzola, and Pear Salad

PREPARATION TIME: 15 minutes

I like to use walnut oil in salads, but it can go bad relatively fast—within a few months. When buying walnut oil, see if it is available in a can or store in a dark, cool place for longer life.

This is a delightful summer salad. Serve with Ratatouille Pizza (page 114) or grilled vegetables.

1/2	cup extra-virgin olive oil
1/3	cup walnut oil
5	tablespoons balsamic vinegar
2	tablespoons lemon juice
1/8	teaspoon salt
1/4	teaspoon pepper
	Red leaf lettuce leaves
1	bunch watercress
2	Comice pears, sliced
1	Newton or Granny Smith apple, sliced
1/4	cup broken walnuts
1	cup Gorgonzola cheese, crumbled

Combine the oils, vinegar, lemon juice, salt, and pepper in a bowl and whisk until blended. On each plate, place a lettuce leaf, some watercress, and a few pear and apple slices. Sprinkle with dressing; add the walnut pieces and crumbled cheese on top.

Serves 4

Each serving provides:

641	Calories	26 g	Carbohydrate
9 g	Protein	489 mg	Sodium
58 g	Fat	21 mg	Cholesterol

Thai Cucumber Salad

PREPARATION TIME: 10 minutes (plus 1 to 2 hours marinating time)

This is another spicy and sweet salad. You can substitute fresh, hot, minced, and seeded pepper for the red pepper flakes if you wish. To make it more authentically Thai, use a dried and soaked de Arbol pepper.

1   cup white wine vinegar
1/4   cup sugar
1/2   teaspoon crushed red pepper flakes
1   cucumber, peeled, cut in half lengthwise, seeded, and thinly sliced
1/2   red onion, cut in half and thinly sliced
1/2   sweet pepper, seeded and julienned

Heat the vinegar and sugar until sugar dissolves, about 5 minutes. Remove from heat and cool. Add red pepper flakes and stir. Place the cucumber, onion, and pepper in a bowl and pour the vinegar mixture over. Marinate for 1 to 2 hours.

Serves 2

Each serving provides:

67	Calories	17 g	Carbohydrate
1 g	Protein	2 mg	Sodium
0 g	Fat	0 mg	Cholesterol

Curried Apple Coleslaw

PREPARATION TIME: 20 minutes

If you wish, substitute a good, quality curry powder for all of the spices except the fresh ginger. I like the mix of apple with curry.

2	cups green cabbage, shredded
2	cups apple, peeled and cut into slivers
1	medium carrot, shredded
1/3	cup raisins
1/8	teaspoon cayenne
1/4	teaspoon *each* cumin, cinnamon
1	teaspoon *each* ground cardamom, coriander
1/2	teaspoon turmeric
1/2	teaspoon paprika
1	teaspoon fresh ginger, grated
2	tablespoons reduced-calorie mayonnaise
2	tablespoons yogurt
2	tablespoons slivered almonds

Combine all ingredients except the almonds in a bowl. Chill, then top with almonds.

Serves 4

Each serving provides:

144	Calories	25 g	Carbohydrate
3 g	Protein	88 mg	Sodium
5 g	Fat	5 mg	Cholesterol

Potato-Jicama Salad

PREPARATION TIME: 30 minutes (plus 1 hour chilling time)

This isn't a spicy salad, and the jicama gives it a nice, fresh flavor. If you must have fire, substitute a teaspoon of minced and seeded jalapeño for the dill.

3	pounds red potatoes, whole, unpeeled
1	sweet onion, cut in half and thinly sliced
1	stalk celery, diced
1	cup jicama, peeled and diced
1/3	cup black olives, sliced
1/3	cup sweet pickle, sliced
1/2	red pepper, seeded and diced
3/4	cup lowfat sour cream
3/4	cup reduced-calorie mayonnaise
1/8	teaspoon salt
1/8	teaspoon pepper
3	teaspoons lemon juice
2	teaspoons Dijon mustard
1	teaspoon fresh dill, chopped

Cook potatoes in boiling water until soft, about 15 minutes. Remove, rinse under cold water, and cut into pieces, but do not peel. Toss with the onion, celery, jicama, olives, pickle, and pepper. Combine the remaining ingredients in a bowl and mix well, then toss with the salad and chill for at least 1 hour.

Serves 6

Each serving provides:

395	Calories	60 g	Carbohydrate
6 g	Protein	531 mg	Sodium
15 g	Fat	32 mg	Cholesterol

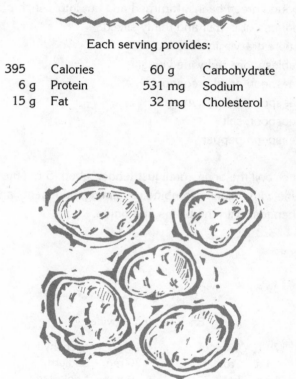

Green Bean Salad

A quick and easy side to many vegetarian entrees.

1	pound green beans, trimmed and cut into 1-inch pieces
1	onion, cut in half and thinly sliced
1/4	cup extra-virgin olive oil
4	tablespoons red wine vinegar
1/2	teaspoon dried oregano
1/4	teaspoon dried thyme
1/8	teaspoon salt
1/8	teaspoon pepper

Steam or boil the beans until just tender, about 5 minutes. Combine with onions. Combine remaining ingredients and mix well, then toss with the beans and onion.

Serves 4

Each serving provides:

178	Calories	14 g	Carbohydrate
3 g	Protein	70 mg	Sodium
14 g	Fat	0 mg	Cholesterol

Jicama Slaw with Cilantro Vinaigrette

PREPARATION TIME: 15 minutes

Jicama's soft flavor nicely offsets the herbs and spices here. In this salad it is matched with a natural ally, cilantro.

3	cups jicama, peeled and grated, or sliced into thin strips
2	carrots, peeled and grated, or sliced into thin strips
1	red pepper, seeded and cut into thin strips
1	small sweet onion, cut in half and thinly sliced
2	tablespoons red wine vinegar
1	tablespoon lemon juice
1/2	cup vegetable oil
2	tablespoons fresh cilantro, chopped
1	teaspoon Dijon mustard
1/4	teaspoon salt
1/4	teaspoon pepper

Combine the jicama, carrots, pepper, and onion in a bowl. Whisk together the remaining ingredients and mix with the jicama mixture.

Serves 4

Each serving provides:

320	Calories	16 g	Carbohydrate
2 g	Protein	189 mg	Sodium
29 g	Fat	0 mg	Cholesterol

Colorful Rice and Black Bean Salad

Preparation Time: 25 minutes (plus 1 hour chilling time)

I enjoy cooking with rice. I like it simple with a little spicy or sweet pepper stirred into it, or more complicated with lots of spices and black beans, as it is in this salad.

2	cups vegetable broth or water
1	cup rice
1	tablespoon white wine vinegar
2	tablespoons extra-virgin olive oil
1/4	teaspoon good-quality chili powder
1	clove garlic, minced
1/4	teaspoon thyme
1/4	teaspoon oregano
1/2	teaspoon Dijon mustard
1	cup black beans, canned okay (see Introduction)
1	red pepper, seeded and julienned
1	green pepper, seeded and julienned
1	jalapeño, seeded and minced
2	tablespoons fresh cilantro, chopped
2	scallions, thinly sliced

Cook the rice in broth or water until done. Meanwhile, combine the vinegar, oil, chili powder, garlic, thyme, oregano, and Dijon in a bowl and whisk together well. Toss cooked rice with the black beans and peppers and then with the dressing. Chill for an hour or longer, then add cilantro and scallions.

Serves 4

Each serving provides:

322	Calories	56 g	Carbohydrate
8 g	Protein	750 mg	Sodium
8 g	Fat	0 mg	Cholesterol

Black Bean Vegetable Salad

PREPARATION TIME: 15 minutes

This is a snap to make and good with many dishes but I like it best with Mexican foods.

2	cups corn, fresh or frozen
2	cups black beans, canned okay (see Introduction)
2	carrots, diced
2	tomatoes, diced
1/2	sweet pepper, seeded and diced
1	teaspoon jalapeño, seeded and minced
	Juice of 2 lemons
1	tablespoon good-quality chili powder
1/8	teaspoon salt

Cook the corn in boiling water for about 3 minutes. Drain and toss with all remaining ingredients.

Serves 4

~~~~~~~~~~

Each serving provides:

217	Calories	46 g	Carbohydrate
11 g	Protein	574 mg	Sodium
1 g	Fat	0 mg	Cholesterol

Cucumber and Dill Salad

This is a sweet, cool salad that goes nicely with hot and spicy dishes. As an alternative, leave out the vinegar and substitute 3/4 cup of lowfat sour cream. But use fresh dill—dried won't work for this salad.

2   cucumbers, peeled, cut in half, and seeded
2   teaspoons sugar
1/4   cup white vinegar
1 1/2 tablespoons fresh dill, chopped

Cut the cucumber into slices and mix with the remaining ingredients. It's better slightly chilled, but tastes fine at room temperature.

Serves 4

Each serving provides:

22	Calories	6 g	Carbohydrate
0 g	Protein	2 mg	Sodium
0 g	Fat	0 mg	Cholesterol

Ziti Vegetable Salad

PREPARATION TIME: 30 minutes

If you don't like these vegetable choices, use any you have on hand. This salad really works as a complete meal.

8	ounces of ziti or other pasta
4	carrots, sliced
2	cups broccoli florets
1/2	red or green bell pepper, seeded and julienned
1	small zucchini, sliced
2	teaspoons Dijon mustard
1	tablespoon red wine vinegar
1/4	cup extra-virgin olive oil
1/2	cup fresh parsley, chives, or basil, chopped
1/4	cup calamata or black olives, seeded and chopped

Cook pasta according to package directions. Microwave or steam the vegetables. Mix together the mustard and vinegar, then slowly add the olive oil, whisking to blend thoroughly. Stir in the herbs. Toss vegetables with the pasta, then add dressing and toss well. Top with olives and serve warm or at room temperature.

Serves 4 as entree, 6 as side dish

Each entree serving provides:

421	Calories	57 g	Carbohydrate
12 g	Protein	281 mg	Sodium
17 g	Fat	0 mg	Cholesterol

Spicy Corn Salad

PREPARATION TIME: 15 minutes (plus 1 hour chilling time)

This bright dish makes a nice luncheon salad. It's at its best with fresh corn.

3	cups corn kernels, fresh or defrosted
1/2	green pepper, seeded and julienned
1/2	red pepper, seeded and julienned
1	jalapeño, seeded and minced
1/2	small red onion, cut in half and thinly sliced
2	tablespoons vegetable oil
1/4	cup wine vinegar
1	teaspoon brown sugar
1/2	teaspoon fresh oregano or 1/4 teaspoon dried
1/4	teaspoon dried thyme

Steam the corn for 2 to 3 minutes, until just tender. Combine the vegetables and mix well. Whisk together the dressing ingredients then toss with the vegetables. Chill at least 1 hour.

Serves 4

Each serving provides:

185	Calories	30 g	Carbohydrate
4 g	Protein	8 mg	Sodium
8 g	Fat	0 mg	Cholesterol

Spicy Pasta and Chickpea Salad

PREPARATION TIME: 20 minutes

Add a dash of hot vinegar (see page 14) or Tabasco sauce if you want to spice up the dressing even more.

10	ounces rotini, cooked according to package directions
20	ounces chickpeas (garbanzo beans), canned okay
1/4	sweet onion, thinly sliced
1	green pepper, seeded and diced
1	red pepper, seeded and diced
1	cup calamata olives, pitted and sliced in half
1	tablespoon fresh parsley, chopped
1/3	cup extra-virgin olive oil
1	tablespoon wine vinegar
1	tablespoon lemon juice
2	cloves garlic, minced
1	teaspoon Dijon mustard
1/2	teaspoon oregano
1/2	teaspoon red pepper flakes
1/8	teaspoon salt
1/4	teaspoon pepper

Combine the first 7 ingredients in a bowl and toss. Whisk together the remaining ingredients and toss with the pasta mix. Serve at room temperature.

Serves 4 as entree, 6 as side dish

Each entree serving provides:

766	Calories	109 g	Carbohydrate
21 g	Protein	1147 mg	Sodium
29 g	Fat	0 mg	Cholesterol

Bean Salad with Orange Vinaigrette

This is a nice salad with barbecued vegetables or any spring or summer dish.

2	tablespoons orange juice
1	tablespoon lemon juice
1/2	teaspoon Dijon mustard
1/2	cup extra-virgin olive oil
1/2	teaspoon fresh thyme or 1/4 teaspoon dried
1/2	teaspoon salt
1	cup red kidney beans, canned okay (see Introduction)
1	cup black beans, canned okay
1	cup garbanzo beans, canned okay
1/2	small red onion, chopped

Combine the first 6 ingredients in a bowl and mix well. Combine the beans and onion and toss. Add vinaigrette and toss. Serve at room temperature.

Serves 4

Each serving provides:

429	Calories	36 g	Carbohydrate
10 g	Protein	778 mg	Sodium
28 g	Fat	0 mg	Cholesterol

3

Soups & Stews

Soups are versatile—they can be a complete meal or a first course for dinner. And soup must be one of the oldest cooking techniques; certainly, soon after the invention of fire people began to make soups.

My favorite thing to add to vegetable soups is basil-cilantro pesto. Use about 30 good-sized basil leaves, blending them with 1/4 cup fresh cilantro, 3 to 4 cloves garlic, 2 to 3 tablespoons pine nuts or walnuts, and enough extra-virgin olive oil to make it just runny—about a cup. (If you don't have cilantro on hand use parsley or make pesto with just basil.) Spoon the pesto into the soup after it is cooked and save the rest for pasta the next day.

Hot soup is especially welcome during Oregon winters which, while usually not arctic, are very damp. That cold, wet air creeps into your bones and a nice homemade soup and bread is the perfect warmup. As you can tell from these recipes, cold soups are another favorite of mine, for warm summer evenings.

Because the recipes in this book take 30 to 35 minutes maximum to prepare, the soups here are simple to make, yet full of flavor.

Vegetable Broth

PREPARATION TIME: 20 minutes (plus 1 hour cooking time)

Vegetable broth is an integral part of many recipes in this book so I'm offering my recipe for making your own. Homemade broth is much better than the canned version. When making broth, remember that a balance of flavors is what you are after. I recommend cutting the vegetables into large chunks for better taste. To improve the flavor, sauté the vegetables lightly before adding them to the water.

2	large onions, coarsely chopped
3	stalks celery, coarsely chopped
1	white turnip, peeled and coarsely chopped
1	whole garlic bulb, unpeeled, quartered
1	bunch parsley
10	carrots, coarsely chopped
3	cups lettuce, chopped
2	teaspoons fresh thyme or 1/2 teaspoon dried
2	teaspoons fresh marjoram or 1/2 teaspoon dried
2	teaspoons pepper
4	quarts water

Place all the vegetables and spices in a large pot and add the water. Bring to a boil then lower heat and simmer, partially covered, until the vegetables become soft (about an hour). Pour the soup through a colander, pressing the vegetables to extract their juices. Discard the solids. Pour the broth through cheesecloth or a strainer. Cool before refrigerating.

Makes about 4 quarts

Each 1 cup serving provides:

10	Calories	2 g	Carbohydrate
1 g	Protein	4 mg	Sodium
0 g	Fat	0 mg	Cholesterol

Pepperpot Soup

PREPARATION TIME: 20 minutes (plus 25 minutes simmering time)

You might want to use 1 red pepper and 1 yellow pepper to add more color to this zesty soup.

2	tablespoons vegetable oil
2	onions, chopped
4	cloves garlic, chopped or minced
2	sweet peppers, seeded and chopped
1	fresh New Mexican pepper, seeded and chopped
2	carrots, peeled and chopped
2	stalks celery, chopped
1	tomato, chopped
1/4	teaspoon ground cayenne
1/2	teaspoon ground cloves
1	teaspoon paprika
6	cups vegetable broth
1	cup cooked rice
2	to 3 tablespoons fresh cilantro, chopped

Sauté the onion and garlic in the oil until soft, about 7 minutes. Add the peppers, carrots, and celery and sauté another 7 minutes. Add the tomatoes and spices and mix well for 1 to 2 minutes. Add the broth and rice and bring to a boil. Reduce heat and simmer 20 to 25 minutes. Stir in the cilantro.

Serves 4

Each serving provides:

241	Calories	39 g	Carbohydrate
5 g	Protein	60 mg	Sodium
8 g	Fat	0 mg	Cholesterol

Dilled Zucchini Soup

PREPARATION TIME: 30 minutes

This soup blends the fresh tastes of dill and zucchini together. It's good with crisp greens and a vinaigrette.

1	tablespoon olive oil
1	onion, chopped
2	cloves garlic, minced
2	medium zucchinis, sliced
2	cups vegetable broth
1	cup water
1	tablespoon fresh dill or 1 teaspoon dried
	Plain yogurt (optional)

Sauté the onion in the oil 2 to 3 minutes in a pot large enough to hold all of the ingredients, then add the garlic for another minute or so. Add the zucchini and sauté 2 to 3 minutes more. Add broth and water. Bring to a boil, reduce heat, cover, and simmer 10 minutes. Add the dill, simmer another 5 minutes. Finish with a spoonful of yogurt and sprinkle dill on top.

Serves 4

Each serving provides:

81	Calories	11 g	Carbohydrate
3 g	Protein	8 mg	Sodium
4 g	Fat	0 mg	Cholesterol

Curried Vegetable Soup

PREPARATION TIME: 15 minutes (plus 30 minutes simmering time)

A spicy soup which works as an entree or a first course.

2	tablespoons vegetable oil
$1/2$	onion, chopped
1	stalk celery, chopped
1	tomato, seeded and chopped
2	carrots, sliced
1	clove garlic, minced
$1/4$	teaspoon *each* cayenne, cumin
1	teaspoon *each* ground cardamom, coriander, dried ginger
$1/2$	teaspoon turmeric
3	cups vegetable broth
3	cups green beans, trimmed and cut in 1-inch pieces
2	tablespoons fresh parsley, minced

Sauté the onion, celery, tomato, carrots, and garlic in the oil 3 to 4 minutes. Add the spices and stir well. Add the broth, bring to a boil, then add beans and simmer for 25 minutes. Stir in the parsley.

Serves 4

Each serving provides:

148	Calories	19 g	Carbohydrate
4 g	Protein	42 mg	Sodium
8 g	Fat	0 mg	Cholesterol

Thai Soup

PREPARATION TIME: 20 minutes

This soup is very spicy, thanks to the fiery Scotch bonnet peppers. (Be sure to use extra caution handling them.) A cooler version without these peppers still has plenty of spice from the jalapeño and ginger.

6	cups vegetable broth
2	tablespoons fresh ginger, grated
1	jalapeño, seeded and cut into strips
1	Scotch bonnet pepper or habanero pepper, seeded and halved
1	pound broccoli, trimmed, peeled, and cut into small pieces
1/2	pound Chinese cabbage (bok choy), shredded
8	mushrooms, thickly sliced
3	tablespoons fresh cilantro, minced
1/4	cup scallions, thinly sliced
2	tablespoons soy sauce
1	lemon, cut into wedges

Combine the broth, ginger, and peppers in a large soup pot and bring to a boil. Add the broccoli, cabbage, and mushrooms, return to a boil then reduce heat and simmer, covered, until the broccoli is cooked but still crisp, about 7 to 8 minutes. Stir in the remaining ingredients and simmer 1 minute more. Remove lemon wedges and Scotch bonnet pepper before serving.

Serves 4

Each serving provides:

85	Calories	16 g	Carbohydrate
7 g	Protein	582 mg	Sodium
1 g	Fat	0 mg	Cholesterol

Curried Corn Soup

PREPARATION TIME: 25 minutes

Curries are a spice lover's best friend. Here, curry is put to good use with fresh corn.

2	tablespoons oil
1/2	small onion, chopped
1	stalk celery, chopped
2	cloves garlic, minced
1 1/2	tablespoons good-quality curry powder
1/8	teaspoon cayenne pepper
1/8	teaspoon ground cumin
4	cups vegetable broth
3	cups corn kernels, fresh or frozen
2	tablespoons fresh parsley, chopped

Sauté the onion and celery in oil 3 to 4 minutes. Add garlic, then stir in the spices and cook another 1 to 2 minutes. Add vegetable broth, bring to a boil, then add the corn and cook 10 minutes. Stir in parsley and serve.

Serves 4

Each serving provides:

191	Calories	30 g	Carbohydrate
5 g	Protein	26 mg	Sodium
8 g	Fat	0 mg	Cholesterol

Cabbage Soup

PREPARATION TIME: 30 minutes (plus 1 hour simmering time)

This is an easy, filling soup, made even better when topped with grated cheese. Serve with plenty of French bread.

2	tablespoons olive oil
2	onions, diced
10	mushrooms, thickly sliced
2	cloves garlic, minced
1/2	cabbage, shredded (about 1 pound, 4 to 5 cups)
2	red or new potatoes, diced
7	cups vegetable broth
1/2	teaspoon thyme
1/2	teaspoon red pepper flakes
1/4	teaspoon salt
1/4	teaspoon pepper
	Grated Swiss, Parmesan, or Gruyère cheese (optional)

In a large pot, sauté onion in oil until soft, about 7 minutes. Add the mushrooms and sauté another 7 to 8 minutes, then add garlic for another 2 minutes. Add remaining ingredients and bring to a boil. Simmer about 1 hour. If desired, remove single servings to bowls, cover with cheese, and place under broiler to melt cheese.

Serves 4

Each serving provides:

220	Calories	36 g	Carbohydrate
6 g	Protein	169 mg	Sodium
8 g	Fat	0 mg	Cholesterol

Zucchini-Basil Soup

PREPARATION TIME: 25 minutes (plus 20 minutes simmering time)

This soup is a tasty first course for pasta entrees or, with French bread, makes a complete meal. If you have it handy, pesto goes nicely with this soup.

2   tablespoons olive oil
1   onion, diced
1   carrot, sliced
1   clove garlic, minced
1   16-ounce can plum tomatoes, crushed
1   zucchini, sliced
1   potato, diced
1/8   teaspoon salt
1/4   teaspoon pepper
1/4   cup fresh basil, chopped
1/4   cup Parmesan cheese
1   tablespoon hot vinegar (optional, recipe on page 14)

Sauté the onion and carrot in oil until onion is soft, about 5 minutes. Add the garlic and tomatoes with their liquid and simmer gently for 10 minutes.

Add the zucchini and potato and enough water to cover, plus an inch or so, and simmer 15 to 20 minutes or until vegetables are tender. Season with salt and pepper, remove from heat, and add basil leaves and Parmesan cheese. Add a little hot vinegar if desired.

Serves 4

Each serving provides:

182	Calories	22 g	Carbohydrate
5 g	Protein	368 mg	Sodium
9 g	Fat	4 mg	Cholesterol

Quick Vegetable Stew

PREPARATION TIME: 30 minutes

This quick and spicy stew is a meal in itself—just serve with bread. If you wish, top it with grated cheddar or Gruyère cheese.

2	tablespoons olive oil
2	onions, chopped
1	jalapeño, seeded and minced
1	teaspoon ground cumin
1	teaspoon dried majoram
1	teaspoon dried coriander
2	cups fresh green beans, cut in 1-inch pieces (thaw if using frozen)
1	zucchini or yellow squash, sliced
1	28-ounce can tomatoes (or 3 cups fresh, peeled, with juice)

Sauté the onions and pepper in olive oil about 5 minutes, until onions begin to soften. Add the spices and green beans and sauté another 3 to 4 minutes. Add the zucchini and tomatoes, cover, and simmer for 15 to 20 minutes, until vegetables are tender.

Serves 4

Each serving provides:

189	Calories	28 g	Carbohydrate
5 g	Protein	349 mg	Sodium
8 g	Fat	0 mg	Cholesterol

Red Pepper Soup

PREPARATION TIME: 15 minutes (plus 30 minutes cooking time)

This bold, red soup is spicy and smooth. Serve with a cooler salad to offset the spiciness and the color.

1	tablespoon olive oil
1	medium onion, diced
1	small carrot, diced
1	stalk celery, diced
4	red peppers, seeded and chopped
1	teaspoon jalapeño, seeded
	Dash of Tabasco or other hot pepper sauce
1	pound red potatoes, peeled and cut into 1/8-inch slices
2	cups vegetable broth
3	cups water
1/2	teaspoon thyme
1/4	teaspoon pepper

Sauté the onion, carrot, and celery in the olive oil until soft, about 8 minutes. Add the remaining ingredients and bring to a boil. Reduce heat and simmer about 30 minutes or until all vegetables are soft. Place in a blender or food processor in batches and puree. Reheat and serve.

Serves 4

Each serving provides:

190	Calories	37 g	Carbohydrate
4 g	Protein	35 mg	Sodium
4 g	Fat	0 mg	Cholesterol

Spicy Corn Chowder

PREPARATION TIME: 30 minutes

A filling soup, enjoy this in the early fall when local corn is at its best. Always good with salads and sandwiches, or as a first course.

4	tablespoons vegetable oil
1	onion, minced
1/2	serrano, seeded and minced
1/2	cup flour
3	cups vegetable broth
1/4	cup dry white wine
1/2	red bell pepper, seeded and minced
2	cups cream
1	teaspoon fresh marjoram, chopped, or 1/2 teaspoon dried
3	cups fresh corn kernels (or frozen and defrosted)
3	tablespoons fresh parsley, chopped
1	cup cheddar cheese, grated

Sauté the serrano and onion in the oil until the onion is soft, about 5 minutes. Add flour and stir for about 3 minutes. Add broth and wine and continue stirring until thickened slightly.

Add the remaining ingredients except cheese, bring to a boil, and simmer 10 to 12 minutes. Remove to a blender or food processor and chop but don't completely puree, then return to saucepan and stir in the cheese.

Serves 4

Each serving provides:

666	Calories	49 g	Carbohydrate
17 g	Protein	189 mg	Sodium
47 g	Fat	107 mg	Cholesterol

Spicy Tomato Soup

PREPARATION TIME: 10 minutes (plus 1 hour chilling time)

Nice to serve with sandwiches or with a summer dinner.

2   cloves garlic, minced
1   to 2 tablespoons jalapeño, seeded and minced
5   cups tomato juice or tomatoes, peeled, seeded,
      and pureed
      Juice of 1/2 lemon
1/2   small sweet onion, finely chopped
1/3   cup fresh cilantro, chopped

Stir all ingredients together and chill for an hour or more.

Serves 4

Each serving provides:

141	Calories	36 g	Carbohydrate
6 g	Protein	1201 mg	Sodium
0 g	Fat	0 mg	Cholesterol

Gazpacho & Creamy Gazpacho

PREPARATION TIME: 20 minutes (plus 1 hour chilling time)

One key to great gazpacho is not to overprocess the vegetables. The vegetables should retain their texture and crunch. If you use a food processor turn the machine on and off to achieve this finely chopped quality. For Creamy Gazpacho: Whisk in 1/4 cup sour cream after the soup has been chilled.

2	sweet onions
1	cucumber, peeled and seeded
2	sweet peppers, seeded
6	small, ripe tomatoes, peeled
2	cloves garlic, minced or chopped
1	jalapeño, seeded and coarsely chopped
2	cups tomato juice
1/2	cup extra-virgin olive oil
1/4	teaspoon salt
1/4	teaspoon pepper

Finely chop the onions, cucumber, sweet peppers, and 3 of the tomatoes and place in a bowl. In a blender or food processor, add the remaining ingredients and puree, then combine the chopped vegetables with the puree. Serve with sour cream if desired, or croutons.

Serves 4

Each serving of regular Gazpacho provides:

368	Calories	29 g	Carbohydrate
5 g	Protein	593 mg	Sodium
28 g	Fat	0 mg	Cholesterol

Cold Tomato and Roasted Pepper Soup

PREPARATION TIME: 15 minutes (plus 1 hour chilling time)

The taste of fresh summer tomatoes blended with roasted peppers and a little spice. Delicious!

2	fresh tomatoes, peeled (see page 4), cored, and cut in half
1	red pepper, roasted (see page 4), stemmed, and seeded
2	cloves garlic, minced
1	jalapeño, seeded and chopped
1/2	small onion, coarsely chopped
4	tablespoons extra-virgin olive oil
3	ice cubes
1	tablespoon fresh cilantro, chopped

Puree all ingredients, except the cilantro. Add 1/4 cup cold water, stir in cilantro, and chill for 1 hour.

Serves 4 as a side dish or starter

~~~~~~~~~~~~~~~~

Each serving provides:

152	Calories	7 g	Carbohydrate
1 g	Protein	8 mg	Sodium
14 g	Fat	0 mg	Cholesterol

Tomato, Pepper, and Cilantro Soup

PREPARATION TIME: 25 minutes (plus 1 hour chilling time)

A perfect cold soup on a hot day.

2   tablespoons olive oil
1   carrot, peeled and chopped
1   sweet onion, chopped
4   ripe tomatoes, peeled and chopped (or 1 28-ounce can whole tomatoes, drained)
1   teaspoon jalapeño, seeded and minced
2   New Mexican peppers, peeled, seeded, and chopped (or one 4-ounce can of green chiles)
2   cloves garlic, minced
5   tablespoons fresh cilantro, chopped

Sauté the carrot and onion in the oil until just softened, about 6 minutes. Add the tomatoes, peppers, and garlic, and sauté gently for 8 to 10 minutes longer. Place all in a blender or food processor along with the cilantro and puree. Chill at least 1 hour before serving.

Serves 4 as a side dish or starter

Each serving provides:

130	Calories	16 g	Carbohydrate
3 g	Protein	25 mg	Sodium
7 g	Fat	0 mg	Cholesterol

Cold, Spicy Cucumber Soup

PREPARATION TIME: 20 minutes (plus 2 hours or more chilling time)

Quick and refreshing in the summer, this is a soup you can make in the morning and it will be ready to serve that night.

4	cucumbers, peeled, seeded, and diced (about 3 1/2 cups)
2	cups yogurt
1 3/4	cups vegetable broth
1	tablespoon white wine vinegar
1/8	teaspoon Tabasco or other hot sauce
2	teaspoons fresh dill, minced
1	tablespoon chives or scallions, finely chopped
1/8	teaspoon white pepper

Place the cucumber pieces in a sieve to drain. Meanwhile, slowly add the broth to the yogurt until smooth, then add remaining ingredients and mix well. Refrigerate until chilled, at least 2 hours.

Serves 4 as a side dish or starter

Each serving provides:

93	Calories	15 g	Carbohydrate
8 g	Protein	94 mg	Sodium
1 g	Fat	2 mg	Cholesterol

Avocado Soup

PREPARATION TIME: 10 minutes (plus 30 minutes chilling time)

A summer soup that makes a beautiful presentation and takes only minutes to make.

2	ripe avocados
1	cup vegetable broth
1/2	cup sour cream
1/2	cup half-and-half
	Fresh ground pepper
1/2	teaspoon ground paprika

Combine all ingredients except paprika in a blender or food processor and blend well. Chill at least 30 minutes (preferably an hour), then top each serving with a dash of paprika.

Serves 4 as a side dish or starter

Each serving provides:

249	Calories	9 g	Carbohydrate
4 g	Protein	36 mg	Sodium
24 g	Fat	22 mg	Cholesterol

4

Companion
Dishes

There is a wonderfully funky grocery store in Portland called Food Front, with one of the greatest produce sections imaginable (without the upscale prices). Here I find many different varieties of fresh peppers and mushrooms, along with celeriac, broccoli rabe, Seckel pears, and many other interesting fruits and vegetables. The store is a co-op and the staff is as different and varied as some of the produce. When you talk to them about the goods, you know these people are proud of their veggies.

Bob Pistone is one Food Front produce peddler who always has ideas on ways to cook different vegetables. Someone like Bob is invaluable for those who like to experiment with untried fresh ingredients. I would imagine that stores like this one can be found in the neighborhoods of many other cities. They are worth seeking out and making that special cross-town trip once in a while.

The side dishes here need no hard-to-find or exotic ingredients, though the recipes cover a broad part of the globe. Most can be found in neighborhood groceries. There are Asian, Mexican, and French influences. With such flavor diversity, you should have no trouble finding companions to use with entrees or salads in this book.

Stir-Fried Red Potatoes

You might serve these spicy potatoes with a salad or two. A green salad, a bean salad, and these potatoes make for a colorful dinner plate.

3	pounds red or new potatoes, whole and unpeeled
3	teaspoons vegetable oil
1	teaspoon red pepper flakes
1	teaspoon ground cumin

Boil the unpeeled potatoes until just soft, 15 to 20 minutes. Cut into cubes. Heat the oil in a large skillet over medium heat. When hot, add the pepper flakes and cumin and stir for about a minute, then add the potatoes, salt, and pepper. Stir-fry until browned on all sides.

Serves 4

Each serving provides:

331	Calories	69 g	Carbohydrate
6 g	Protein	16 mg	Sodium
4 g	Fat	0 mg	Cholesterol

Asparagus with Ginger-Lemon Dressing

PREPARATION TIME: 10 minutes

Light lemon and ginger complement the delicate taste of asparagus. If you want a little different taste, buy very thin stalks, steam them, then fry the asparagus over medium heat in a butter and oil mixture until the tips begin to turn black.

1 1/2 teaspoons fresh ginger, grated
1/8 cup fresh lemon juice
1/4 cup olive oil
2 teaspoons walnut oil
1 scallion (white part), minced
1/2 teaspoon fresh dill, minced, or 1/4 teaspoon dried
1 pound asparagus, steamed or microwaved

Place the ginger and lemon juice in a bowl. Slowly whisk in the olive and walnut oils until emuslified. Stir in the scallion and dill, then pour over cooked asparagus.

Serves 4

Each serving provides:

162	Calories	5 g	Carbohydrate
2 g	Protein	10 mg	Sodium
16 g	Fat	0 mg	Cholesterol

Hot, Spicy Rice and Raisins

PREPARATION TIME: 25 minutes

Curried rice is a regular at my table. When I don't know what to cook, we have a quick curry (sometimes with interesting vegetable combinations, since I tend to use what's on hand when I make this). If you like, add a sliced zucchini or other vegetable to the onions and peppers after they have cooked 3 to 4 minutes. This is hot, but a milder version without the hot pepper or with less cayenne is just as delicious.

1 1/2 cups rice
1/3   cup vegetable oil
1   teaspoon *each* ground cayenne, cumin, turmeric
1/2   teaspoon *each* ground cloves, cardamom
1   sweet red or green bell pepper, seeded and julienned
1/2   onion, chopped
1/2   teaspoon jalapeño or other hot pepper, seeded and minced
1 1/2 teaspoons fresh ginger, grated
1/2   cup raisins

Cook the rice. Heat the oil in a large skillet over medium-low heat and add the spices (except the ginger). Mix well, then add the red or green pepper, onion, and hot pepper and continue to cook, stirring frequently, until the peppers and onion are soft, 10 to 12 minutes. Add ginger, then stir the cooked rice into the skillet, before adding the raisins. Mix well.

Serves 4

Each serving provides:

494	Calories	74 g	Carbohydrate
6 g	Protein	8 mg	Sodium
20 g	Fat	0 mg	Cholesterol

Simple Summer Vegetables

PREPARATION TIME: 20 minutes

This quick, Provençal-style vegetable dish brings out three tastes of summer, blending fresh rosemary, zucchini, and sweet onion.

3	tablespoons olive oil
2	zucchinis, sliced
1	large sweet onion, cut in half and thinly sliced
1	tablespoon fresh rosemary, chopped
1	tablespoon fresh thyme, chopped, or 1 1/2 teaspoons dried
1	clove garlic
1	cup Parmesan cheese

Sauté zucchini and onion in the olive oil until very soft, about 12 minutes. For the last minute or two of cooking, add the rosemary and thyme.

Meanwhile, cut the garlic clove in half and use it to rub the bottom of a casserole dish. Spread the zucchini and onion mix in the casserole dish, spread the Parmesan on top and broil until the cheese has melted completely.

Serves 4

Each serving provides:

236	Calories	12 g	Carbohydrate
11 g	Protein	376 mg	Sodium
17 g	Fat	16 mg	Cholesterol

Tomatoes with Parsley

PREPARATION TIME: 15 minutes

*Here is a simple, beautiful dish that captures the fresh taste of
summer tomatoes.*

1	clove garlic, minced
1/2	cup extra-virgin olive oil
3	tablespoons wine vinegar
	Salt and pepper to taste
3	cups packed fresh parsley
1/2	cup Parmesan cheese
4	medium vine-ripened tomatoes

Process garlic, olive oil, vinegar, salt, and pepper in a blender
or shake in a covered jar. Pour dressing over parsley. Add
Parmesan cheese and mix well. Put tomato slices in glass
bowl. Add parsley-cheese mixture and toss well.

Serves 4

Each serving provides:

361	Calories	15 g	Carbohydrate
9 g	Protein	402 mg	Sodium
31 g	Fat	8 mg	Cholesterol

Gruyère Potatoes

PREPARATION TIME: 25 minutes (plus 1 hour cooking time)

Potatoes with cheese and cream may not make the lowfat list but my version of this traditional French dish is a wonderfully rich mixture of potatoes and cheese.

1	tablespoon melted butter, or oil
2	tablespoons fresh parsley, chopped
1	cup cream
2	baking potatoes, peeled and sliced
2	cloves garlic, minced
1	cup Gruyère cheese, shredded

Preheat oven to 350°. Brush a baking dish with the butter or oil. Mix the parsley and the cream together. Layer half of the potatoes in the dish and sprinkle with the garlic and half of the cheese. Pour half of the cream-parsley mixture over the potatoes. Repeat the process with the remaining ingredients and top with salt and pepper if desired. Bake about 1 hour or until brown.

Serves 4

Each serving provides:

366	Calories	27 g	Carbohydrate
12 g	Protein	134 mg	Sodium
24 g	Fat	79 mg	Cholesterol

Quick Mexican Vegetables

PREPARATION TIME: 15 minutes

These go nicely with any Mexican dish, or simply serve with rice and beans.

3	tablespoons vegetable oil
1	tablespoon unsalted butter
1	sweet onion, thinly sliced
1	red bell pepper, seeded and julienned
1	zucchini, cut into 3-inch strips
1/2	pound jicama, cut into 3-inch strips
1	small chayote squash, halved, seeded, and cut into matchsticks
1/4	teaspoon ground cumin
1/8	teaspoon cayenne
3	tablespoons fresh cilantro, chopped
	Juice of 1/2 lime

Heat the oil and butter in a skillet and add remaining ingredients, except cilantro and lime juice. Stir-fry until crisp tender. Stir in cilantro and sprinkle with lime juice.

Serves 6

Each serving provides:

198	Calories	17 g	Carbohydrate
3 g	Protein	9 mg	Sodium
14 g	Fat	8 mg	Cholesterol

Spicy Greens and Beans

PREPARATION TIME: 25 minutes

An unusual mixture of fresh greens and beans with the addition of spicy red pepper flakes. You might try it when serving soup as a main dish.

1	tablespoon sesame or peanut oil
1	small red or green bell pepper, chopped
1	clove garlic, minced
1	tablespoon fresh ginger, grated
1¹/2	pounds bok choy, chopped
1	cup kidney beans or black beans, canned okay (see Introduction, page 3)
¹/8	teaspoon red pepper flakes
1	teaspoon soy sauce or tamari, or to taste

Heat the oil in a wok or skillet and sauté the bell pepper over medium heat for about 5 minutes. Stir in the garlic and ginger, then add bok choy and stir-fry for 2 minutes. Add beans, red pepper flakes, and soy sauce and continue to stir-fry for 4 to 5 minutes.

Serves 4

Each serving provides:

113	Calories	15 g	Carbohydrate
6 g	Protein	415 mg	Sodium
4 g	Fat	0 mg	Cholesterol

Spicy Green Beans

The roasted peppers give an almost smoky flavor to the beans.

2   tomatoes
1   tablespoon vegetable oil
1   onion, chopped
3   jalapeños, seeded, roasted (see Introduction, page 4), and finely chopped
1   clove garlic, minced
1   pound green beans, trimmed and cut in 1-inch pieces

Place the tomatoes in boiling water for a few seconds, remove, and place in cold water to stop cooking. Peel and chop. Sauté the onion in oil until soft, add the jalapeños and garlic and sauté for 2 more minutes. Meanwhile, cook the green beans in boiling water for 12 minutes, until crisp-tender, or steam for 15 to 16 minutes. Drain, then add the beans to the sauté and cook a minute longer.

Serves 4

Each serving provides:

123	Calories	20 g	Carbohydrate
4 g	Protein	12 mg	Sodium
4 g	Fat	0 mg	Cholesterol

Rice with Cheese

This rice is a nice match for vegetable dishes and vegetable salads.

2	tablespoons vegetable oil
1/2	onion, chopped
1/2	cup red pepper, seeded and chopped
1	jalapeño, seeded and minced
1	clove garlic, minced
1	14-ounce can tomatoes, undrained and chopped
1/4	cup water
1	cup rice
2	tablespoons fresh cilantro, chopped
1/2	cup grated Parmesan cheese

Sauté the onion, peppers, and garlic in oil over medium-low heat until soft, about 10 minutes. Add the tomatoes and their juice, the water, and the rice. Bring to a boil, cover, and reduce heat. Simmer 20 minutes or until moisture is absorbed. Stir in the cilantro and cheese.

Serves 4

Each serving provides:

318	Calories	46 g	Carbohydrate
9 g	Protein	362 mg	Sodium
11 g	Fat	0 mg	Cholesterol

Sweet & Hot Carrots

PREPARATION TIME: 15 minutes

This quick and easy side dish goes with a great many things, from rice dishes to casseroles.

1	pound carrots, peeled and sliced 1/8-inch thick
1/4	cup extra-virgin olive oil
1	teaspoon ground cumin
1	teaspoon brown sugar
1/4	teaspoon ground cayenne
3	cloves garlic, minced
2	teaspoons fresh parsley, minced

Steam the carrots until just tender. Mix olive oil, cumin, sugar, cayenne, and garlic together in a bowl. Pour over the carrots and toss well. Add parsley and toss again.

Serves 4

Each serving provides:

180	Calories	14 g	Carbohydrate
2 g	Protein	79 mg	Sodium
14 g	Fat	0 mg	Cholesterol

Snappy Garbanzos

PREPARATION TIME: 10 minutes (plus 30 minutes simmering time)

Serve this garbanzo dish with cornbread.

1	tablespoon olive oil
1	onion, chopped
2	cloves garlic, minced
2	cups garbanzo beans, drained, canned okay (see Introduction)
1/2	teaspoon red pepper flakes
1	teaspoon dried oregano
1	28-ounce can tomatoes or 1 pound fresh, peeled and chopped with juice
1	cup tomato juice
1/4	teaspoon salt
1/2	teaspoon pepper

In a Dutch oven, heat the oil and sauté the onion until almost soft, then add the remaining ingredients. Bring to a boil, then reduce and simmer about 30 minutes.

Serves 4

Each serving provides:

251	Calories	45 g	Carbohydrate
8 g	Protein	941 mg	Sodium
6 g	Fat	0 mg	Cholesterol

Mediterranean Rice

PREPARATION TIME: 25 minutes

Bringing together many tastes of the Mediterranean, this rice is good with a salad or on its own—and it's great reheated the next day.

1	cup rice
1	red or green bell pepper, seeded and diced
2	tablespoons olive oil
3	cloves garlic, minced
1	teaspoon thyme
1	teaspoon oregano
1/4	teaspoon red pepper flakes
1/8	teaspoons salt
1/4	teaspoon pepper
2	cups tomatoes, peeled with juice, or 1 14-ounce can with 1/3 cup juice
1/2	cup calamata olives, pitted and cut in half
	Crumbled feta cheese (optional)

Cook the rice in 2 1/4 cups of water until done, about 17 minutes. In a skillet, sauté the pepper in oil for 2 to 3 minutes, then add the garlic and spices. Stir in the tomatoes with juice and olives and simmer 3 to 4 minutes. Stir in the rice and combine until mixed well. Top with cheese if desired.

Serves 4

Each serving provides:

297	Calories	46 g	Carbohydrate
5 g	Protein	396 mg	Sodium
11 g	Fat	0 mg	Cholesterol

Gingered Black Beans

Serve this spicy bean dish over rice or alongside Mexican or Asian entrees.

1	large onion, chopped
3	tablespoons olive oil
3	cloves garlic, minced
1	teaspoon jalapeño, seeded and minced
1 1/2	tablespoons fresh ginger, grated
1/4	teaspoon ground allspice
3	16-ounce cans black beans, rinsed and drained, or about 4 cups fresh, soaked overnight and drained
1/2	cup orange juice
1/4	cup water

Sauté the onion in the oil until soft, 5 to 6 minutes. Add the garlic and pepper and sauté 2 to 3 minutes, add the ginger and allspice and stir another 2 minutes. Stir in the beans, juice, and water, and cook over low heat about 15 minutes.

Serves 6

Each serving provides:

152	Calories	18 g	Carbohydrate
5 g	Protein	324 mg	Sodium
7 g	Fat	0 mg	Cholesterol

Simple & Spicy
Zucchini Fritters

PREPARATION TIME: 25 minutes

This style of fritter is popular in France and throughout the Mediterranean. Try serving these with pasta dishes.

2   zucchinis, grated and pressed to remove excess liquid
2   cloves garlic, minced
1/2 teaspoon dried thyme
1/3 cup freshly grated Parmesan cheese
     Dash of Tabasco or other hot pepper sauce
4   tablespoons extra-virgin olive oil

Combine all ingredients and half of the olive oil in a bowl. Shape into patties. Heat the remaining oil in a skillet and brown patties on both sides.

Serves 6

Each serving provides:

115	Calories	3 g	Carbohydrate
3 g	Protein	85 mg	Sodium
11 g	Fat	4 mg	Cholesterol

Spanish Rice

Every cook who enjoys Mexican food has a favorite recipe for Spanish rice, it seems, and here is mine. It's easy to assemble and you can let it cook while you prepare the tacos or enchiladas.

1	medium onion, finely chopped
1/2	red or green bell pepper, seeded and finely chopped
1	teaspoon jalapeño, seeded and minced, or 1/2 teaspoon ground cayenne
2	cloves garlic, minced
1/4	cup extra-virgin olive oil
1	cup long-grain rice
2	cups vegetable broth or water
1	cup tomato sauce
1/2	teaspoon ground cumin

Sauté the onion and peppers in oil until onion is soft, about 5 minutes. Add garlic and mix well. Stir in the rice, stirring for 4 to 5 minutes over medium heat. Add the remaining ingredients, bring to a boil, then simmer, covered, for 20 minutes or until liquid is absorbed.

Serves 4

Each serving provides:

342	Calories	49 g	Carbohydrate
5 g	Protein	374 mg	Sodium
14 g	Fat	0 mg	Cholesterol

Carrot and Cilantro Rice

PREPARATION TIME: 20 minutes

Here's a quick side dish to give rice both color and crunch.

1 1/2 cups rice
3 1/4 cups vegetable broth or water
1 1/2 cups raw carrot, grated
1/2   cup green onions, finely chopped
1/2   teaspoon cumin
1/8   teaspoon cayenne
2   tablespoons fresh cilantro, finely chopped

Cook rice in the vegetable broth or water for about 17 minutes, or until all of the liquid is absorbed. Stir all ingredients into the rice.

Serves 4

Each serving provides:

288	Calories	63 g	Carbohydrate
6 g	Protein	24 mg	Sodium
1 g	Fat	0 mg	Cholesterol

Teriyaki Mushrooms and Peppers

PREPARATION TIME: 20 minutes

Delicious, of course, with oriental dishes but also good as an entree over a bed of rice.

1	pound crimini, shiitake, or button mushrooms, quartered
1	red or green bell pepper, seeded and cut into squares
	Sesame oil
5	tablespoons soy sauce
2	tablespoons sugar
1 1/2	tablespoons fresh ginger, minced
1 1/2	tablespoons rice wine or rice wine vinegar

Thread the mushrooms and peppers onto skewers and brush lightly with sesame oil. Grill over a charcoal fire or broil in a baking dish 4 to 5 minutes, turning frequently. Combine remaining ingredients in a saucepan and stir to dissolve sugar. Heat to boiling, remove from heat, and transfer to a serving bowl. Spoon a little sauce over skewers and serve the remainder for dipping.

Serves 4

Each serving provides:

96	Calories	15 g	Carbohydrate
4 g	Protein	1305 mg	Sodium
3 g	Fat	0 mg	Cholesterol

Lemon Herb Rice

PREPARATION TIME: 20 minutes

Fresh herbs are best in this dish. A fine accompaniment to vegetable dishes.

1   cup rice
2¼   cups vegetable broth or water
2   teaspoons *each* fresh thyme, oregano, tarragon, and
       chives or 1 teaspoon *each* dried
1   tablespoon fresh lemon juice
2   teaspoons white wine vinegar

Cook the rice in the liquid about 20 minutes, or until all liquid is absorbed. Meanwhile, mince the herbs. Combine the herbs, lemon juice, and vinegar with the rice and serve.

Serves 4

Each serving provides:

178	Calories	39 g	Carbohydrate
4 g	Protein	5 mg	Sodium
0 g	Fat	0 mg	Cholesterol

Spicy Potato Pancakes

PREPARATION TIME: 25 minutes

My mother used to make potato pancakes for breakfast out of last night's leftover mashed potatoes. I've come up with this recipe for spicy and quick fresh pancakes, but I'm not sure they're ever as good as hers—or the memory of hers.

2	eggs
1	pound potatoes, peeled and grated (about 2 cups)
1/2	teaspoon salt
1/8	teaspoon pepper
1	teaspoon red pepper flakes
2	tablespoons flour
1/2	small onion, grated (about 1/3 cup)
1	tablespoon cream or milk
	Vegetable oil

Beat the eggs and mix with the potatoes, then mix with the remaining ingredients except the oil, until well combined. Heat enough oil in a skillet to cover the bottom of the pan. Add 3 tablespoons or so of batter and spread into a thin pancake. Fry until brown, 2 to 3 minutes per side.

Serves 4

Each serving provides:

216	Calories	25 g	Carbohydrate
6 g	Protein	305 mg	Sodium
11 g	Fat	110 mg	Cholesterol

Saucy Carrots and Green Beans

PREPARATION TIME: 15 minutes

When you are serving something complicated, this simple dish of fresh herbs and easy flavors is very nice on the side.

3   carrots, peeled and julienned
2   cups green beans, trimmed and cut into 1-inch pieces
1   tablespoon Dijon mustard
1   teaspoon tarragon vinegar
3   tablespoons fresh parsley, finely chopped
1   teaspoon fresh tarragon, or 1/2 teaspoon dried
3   tablespoons extra-virgin olive oil
1/2   teaspoon lemon juice

Steam the vegetables until crisp-tender and toss together. Mix the mustard, vinegar, parsley, and tarragon in a bowl. Slowly add the olive oil, whisking it in to mix. Add lemon juice, whisk thoroughly, then pour over vegetables.

Serves 4

Each serving provides:

143	Calories	11 g	Carbohydrate
2 g	Protein	130 mg	Sodium
11 g	Fat	0 mg	Cholesterol

Green Beans in Hazelnut Butter

PREPARATION TIME: 15 minutes

The Northwest has an abundance of hazelnuts and I enjoy adding them to many dishes. This may not win the low-cholesterol award but the combination of the crisp-tender fresh beans, butter, and nuts is heavenly.

1   pound green beans, trimmed
3   tablespoons unsalted butter
1/3   cup hazelnuts, skinned and chopped

Cook the beans in boiling water until just tender, about 3 minutes. Drain and place in a pot of cold water to stop the cooking process. Melt the butter in a large skillet and add the beans. Stir-fry for 2 minutes, then add the hazelnuts and stir to combine well. Remove from heat and serve.

Serves 4

Each serving provides:

183	Calories	11 g	Carbohydrate
3 g	Protein	5 mg	Sodium
16 g	Fat	25 mg	Cholesterol

Pineapple-Curry Rice

PREPARATION TIME: 20 minutes

This sweet and spicy dish is a little too intense as a dish on its own. Serve with shish kabobs or a stir-fry.

1/4 teaspoon *each* cardamom, turmeric, ground coriander, cumin, cayenne
1/8 teaspoon *each* ground cloves, nutmeg
1/2 teaspoon sweet paprika
2 cloves garlic, minced
1 1/2 teaspoons fresh ginger, grated
1 tablespoon brown sugar
1/4 cup pineapple juice
1/2 cup pineapple, finely diced
Cooked rice

Stir the spices together in a small skillet on low heat for a minute or two. Add the garlic, ginger, sugar, and pineapple juice, and cook on medium heat, stirring frequently, for 5 to 7 minutes. Remove from heat and add the pineapple. Serve on the side with the rice.

Serves 4

Each serving not including rice provides:

55	Calories	14 g	Carbohydrate
0 g	Protein	4 mg	Sodium
0 g	Fat	0 mg	Cholesterol

Raw Vegetables with Soy-Ginger Sauce

PREPARATION TIME: 30 minutes

Raw vegetables covered with a sauce go nicely with many Asian dishes. Use the seasonal, fresh vegetables you have on hand.

1/4	cup tamari or soy sauce
1/4	cup water
1	teaspoon sherry
1 1/2	tablespoons fresh ginger, grated
1	teaspoon vegetable oil
1/2	teaspoon sugar
3	carrots, peeled and cut into sticks
1	head broccoli or cauliflower florets
6	button mushrooms

Whisk the tamari or soy sauce, water, sherry, ginger, oil, and sugar together; let stand for 30 minutes. Meanwhile, slice or chop the vegetables, and toss together. Strain to remove ginger strings from sauce and pour over raw vegetables.

Serves 4

Each serving provides:

80	Calories	13 g	Carbohydrate
5 g	Protein	1057 mg	Sodium
2 g	Fat	0 mg	Cholesterol

Curried Fried Rice

PREPARATION TIME: 15 minutes

*Fried rice works best when the rice is cold so this is an ideal
dish for using last night's rice. It's an excuse for making too
much rice tonight so you can have curried fried rice tomorrow!
Be sure to separate the cold rice with a fork before stirring in.*

5   tablespoons vegetable broth or water
1   tablespoon soy sauce
1   teaspoon fresh ginger, grated
1/2   teaspoon salt
2   tablespoons vegetable oil
1   small onion, finely chopped
2   carrots, peeled and finely chopped
2   tablespoons good-quality curry powder
1   cup fresh peas steamed 2 to 3 minutes, or frozen peas, thawed
3 1/2 cups cold, cooked rice

Combine the first 4 ingredients in a bowl and set aside. Heat
the oil in a wok or skillet over medium-high, add the onion and
carrots and stir-fry 3 to 4 minutes. Add the curry powder, stir
in well, then add the peas and stir-fry just until heated, about a
minute or two. Add rice, stir in well to mix, then add sauce.
Remove from heat and toss to mix well.

Serves 4

Each serving provides:

367	Calories	65 g	Carbohydrate
8 g	Protein	581 mg	Sodium
8 g	Fat	0 mg	Cholesterol

5

Pasta and
Pizza

As every cook-on-the-run knows, pasta is a fast and easy way to the dinner table. These pasta dishes use fresh ingredients and sometimes raw vegetables to bring color, flavor, and good nutrition to your meal.

We never ate much pasta when I was growing up. It was usually meat and potatoes. I remember pizza as a rare treat for us. Of course, we ate our share of processed foods as well, including the ubiquitous, odd-tasting fish sticks. Now, as cooks demand higher quality, we've come full circle, back to shopping for fresh vegetables and fresh breads the way our grandparents did because, while those '50s and '60s convenience foods were convenient, they didn't taste very good.

One simple taste-enhancer is to flavor your olive oil before you toss it with the pasta. For example, a sprig of fresh rosemary added to oil over low heat for 20 or 30 minutes will infuse the oil with the flavor of that herb. The rosemary-infused oil nicely complements noodles tossed with fresh vegetables and mild herbs. The same is true for other ingredients including peppers, which can infuse the oil with heat, as they do in the Spaghetti with Hot Pepper Sauce. Peppers can also add flavor to the water you use to cook the pasta, and thereby add flavor to the pasta. The very spicy Scotch bonnet peppers are used for that purpose in the Ziti with Herbs recipe.

Serving a cheese bread or bread rubbed with oil and garlic goes well with many pasta dishes, of course. For cheese bread, I just slice a baguette, rub the slices with butter or oil, rub them again with minced garlic, sprinkle on fresh Parmesan, then broil them briefly to melt the cheese.

For the spicier pastas you may want to add a few slices of cold carrots or cucumber on the plate to refresh the palate. If the heat of a dish is too much for the kids, consider recipes where you can add the spice toward the end, and make two versions, one hot and one mild. Also remember, fresh herbs and spices can usually be added later than dried ones.

In the Sauces, Salsas, and Dressings section you can find a recipe for pizza sauce (page 23) that may be added to any pizzas. Just cover the crust with the pizza sauce after you use the olive oil, then add the toppings of your choice.

Lime-Curry Orzo

PREPARATION TIME: 25 minutes

I like to have a simple, green salad with this somewhat un-usual pasta dish.

8	ounces orzo or other small pasta
5	tablespoons vegetable oil
1/3	cup onion, minced
1	stalk celery, thinly sliced
1/4	teaspoon *each* turmeric, ground coriander, cardamom, and sweet paprika
1/8	teaspoon *each* ground cumin, cloves, and cayenne
2	tablespoons fresh ginger, grated
2	tablespoons lime juice
1	teaspoon salt
1/2	teaspoon pepper
12	calamata or black olives
1/2	cup crumbled feta cheese (optional)

Cook the orzo according to package directions. In 1 tablespoon of the oil, sauté the onion over low heat for 5 minutes or until soft, adding the celery for the last few minutes. Add the spices except the ginger, salt, and pepper, mixing well. Remove from heat and stir in the ginger, lime juice, salt, pepper, olives, and remaining 4 tablespoons of oil. Top with the cheese if desired.

Serves 4

Each serving provides:

382	Calories	45 g	Carbohydrate
8 g	Protein	546 mg	Sodium
19 g	Fat	0 mg	Cholesterol

Lemon Spaghetti

PREPARATION TIME: 20 minutes

This is a simple pasta to serve at the end of a busy day, and easy to make since it calls for ingredients you are likely to have on hand. Garlic bread or focaccia goes well with it.

1	pound spaghetti
1	tablespoon olive oil
3	zucchinis, sliced
2	tablespoons fresh basil, chopped, or 2 teaspoons dried
7	mushrooms, sliced
3	to 4 cloves garlic, minced
	Juice of 1 1/2 lemons
1	cup fresh Parmesan or pecorino cheese, grated

Cook pasta according to package directions. Heat the olive oil in a skillet and add the zucchini and basil. Cook over medium heat for about 5 minutes, then add mushrooms and cook another 5 minutes. Add garlic, stir, and cook for 2 minutes, then pour in the lemon juice and remove from heat. Toss with the cooked and drained pasta; top with the cheese.

Serves 4

Each serving provides:

604	Calories	98 g	Carbohydrate
26 g	Protein	382 mg	Sodium
12 g	Fat	16 mg	Cholesterol

Penne with Calamata Olives

PREPARATION TIME: 20 minutes

The fresh taste of the spices together with the strong olives gives this dish a nice Mediterranean taste. If you're feeling Italian use the Parmesan; if it's Greek use feta!

1	pound penne pasta
2	tablespoons olive oil
1/2	onion, minced
3	cloves garlic, minced
1/2	cup calamata olives, pitted and chopped
1	teaspoon fresh rosemary, chopped, or 1/2 teaspoon dried
1	teaspoon fresh thyme, or 1/2 teaspoon dried
1/3	cup white wine
1/2	cup grated Parmesan or feta cheese

Cook the penne according to package directions. Meanwhile, sauté the onion in olive oil until soft, about 5 minutes. Add the garlic, olives, rosemary, thyme, and wine and bring to a boil. Turn heat to low and simmer 3 to 4 minutes. Toss with pasta, and then with the cheese.

Serves 4

Each serving provides:

613	Calories	95 g	Carbohydrate
20 g	Protein	506 mg	Sodium
15 g	Fat	8 mg	Cholesterol

Ratatouille Pizza

PREPARATION TIME: 30 minutes

A quick pizza that will get your kids to love vegetables. Use a good-quality bread for best results—I prefer unbaked focaccia, available in many stores.

1	prepared focaccia bread or pizza crust
3	tablespoons olive oil
1	small onion, chopped
2	medium zucchinis, sliced
2	medium red peppers, seeded and sliced into thin strips
1	tablespoon dried basil
1	teaspoon dried oregano
1	teaspoon dried dill
3	cloves garlic, minced
	Parmesan cheese

Preheat oven to 400° or the temperature recommended for the packaged bread. Rub the bread with 1 tablespoon of olive oil and set aside. Heat the remaining 2 tablespoons of olive oil in a skillet and add the onion, zucchini, and red pepper. Stir in the spices and sauté until soft, about 10 minutes. Add the garlic for the last half of cooking. Pour the vegetables over the bread and bake 10 to 15 minutes, or according to the package instructions. Sprinkle Parmesan on top for the last 4 to 5 minutes of cooking.

Serves 4

Each serving provides:

276	Calories	42 g	Carbohydrate
10 g	Protein	436 mg	Sodium
7 g	Fat	4 mg	Cholesterol

Penne with Peppers

PREPARATION TIME: 20 minutes

Colorful and full of flavor, this pasta goes especially well with a sweet salad.

3	tablespoons olive oil
1	red bell pepper, seeded and julienned
1	yellow bell pepper, seeded and julienned
1	green bell pepper, seeded and julienned
2	cloves garlic, minced
1	medium zucchini, sliced
2	teaspoons fresh thyme or 1 teaspoon dried
10	ounces penne or other hollow pasta
3/4	cup ricotta cheese
3/4	cup plain yogurt

Sauté peppers in the oil over low-medium heat for 2 to 3 minutes. Add garlic, zucchini, and thyme and sauté another 5 to 6 minutes. Cook the pasta according to package directions. Combine the cheese and yogurt in a blender and process until smooth. Stir the cheese into the pepper mixture and then toss with the pasta.

Serves 4

Each serving provides:

486	Calories	69 g	Carbohydrate
19 g	Protein	96 mg	Sodium
16 g	Fat	15 mg	Cholesterol

Fettuccine with Garlic and Zucchini

<small>PREPARATION TIME:</small> 20 minutes

A quick, simple, and flavorful pasta with wonderful summer flavors. Serve with a green salad tossed with a vinaigrette.

2	medium zucchinis, julienned
1/3	cup extra-virgin olive oil
4	cloves garlic, minced
2	tablespoons fresh thyme or 1 tablespoon dried
1	pound fettuccine or other pasta
	Parmesan cheese (optional)

Steam the zucchini until just tender. Heat the olive oil over low heat and add the garlic, cooking gently so it does not brown, about 10 minutes. Meanwhile, cook the pasta and drain. Toss with the other ingredients and top with Parmesan cheese, if desired.

Serves 4

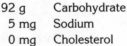

Each serving provides:

616	Calories	92 g	Carbohydrate
16 g	Protein	5 mg	Sodium
20 g	Fat	0 mg	Cholesterol

Fettuccine with Peas and Peppers

A rich pasta with plenty of color. You might consider a butter and oil mix for the sauté.

1	cup fresh peas or pea pods
4	tablespoons butter or vegetable oil
1/2	red bell pepper, seeded and julienned
4	mushrooms, sliced
12	ounces fettuccine
2	tablespoons heavy cream
2	tablespoons fresh chives or scallions, minced
1/3	cup fresh Parmesan cheese, grated

Steam or microwave peas or pea pods until tender. Heat the butter or oil in a skillet and sauté pepper 2 to 3 minutes. Add the mushrooms and stir, heating for another 3 to 4 minutes until just cooked. Cook fettuccine according to package directions. Add the cream, chives, and Parmesan cheese to the fettuccine and mix well. Fold in the peas, peppers, and mushrooms.

Serves 4

Each serving provides:

534	Calories	74 g	Carbohydrate
17 g	Protein	288 mg	Sodium
19 g	Fat	49 mg	Cholesterol

Spaghetti Verdura

This mix uses mustard to give the sauce a dressing effect. The shallots give it a rich flavor.

5	tablespoons extra-virgin olive oil
3	shallots, minced
1	clove garlic, minced
3	tablespoons Dijon mustard
2	zucchinis, cut in half lengthwise, then sliced
1/2	pound asparagus, cut into 1-inch pieces
1	pound spaghetti, cooked
2	tablespoons scallions or chives, chopped
1/8	teaspoon pepper

Sauté the shallots and garlic in 2 tablespoons of the oil until soft, about 5 minutes. Add remaining 3 tablespoons of oil and mustard and mix well. Steam or microwave the zucchini and asparagus until crisp tender. Toss the cooked pasta with the dressing to coat, then add vegetables and scallions and toss again. Season with pepper.

Serves 4

Each serving provides:

652	Calories	99 g	Carbohydrate
19 g	Protein	316 mg	Sodium
21 g	Fat	0 mg	Cholesterol

Peppers Stuffed with Pasta and Cheese

PREPARATION TIME: 20 minutes (plus 35 minutes baking time)

Orzo is superior to rice for stuffing since it maintains a little of its own flavor in process. All you need to serve with this is bread.

8	ounces orzo or other small pasta
6	large red or green sweet peppers
1/8	teaspoon salt
1/4	teaspoon pepper
1	tablespoon extra-virgin olive oil
1/2	cup calamata olives, pitted
1/4	cup parsley, chopped
2	teaspoons pine nuts
1/8	teaspoon Tabasco or other hot sauce
1/2	pound goat cheese or cubed mozzarella

Preheat oven to 400°. Cook the pasta 2/3 of the time recommended on the package. Cut tops off the peppers and remove seeds and veins. Mix together the salt, pepper, and oil, then spread the mixture on the inside of the peppers. Chop the olives and mix with parsley and pine nuts. Drain the pasta and combine with olive mixture and hot sauce. Stir in cheese, then spoon the mix into the peppers. Place in an oiled or greased baking pan and cover with foil. Cook 10 minutes, remove foil, and cook another 25 minutes.

Serves 4

Each serving provides:

474	Calories	52 g	Carbohydrate
20 g	Protein	595 mg	Sodium
21 g	Fat	26 mg	Cholesterol

Mushroom-Ginger Pasta

PREPARATION TIME: 25 minutes

Ginger is good for you. It has been used for centuries in Asia and Africa for a variety of stomach ailments, and—guess what—Western science is beginning to agree that folk medicine works. I simply love the taste and smell of fresh ginger.

1	tablespoon olive oil
1	onion, cut in half and thinly sliced
1	pound mushrooms, sliced
1/2	cup dry white wine
1	cup sour cream
1	cup yogurt
2	teaspoons fresh ginger, grated
1	pound fettuccine, cooked

Sauté the onion in oil for 3 minutes. Remove onions, then add mushrooms to the oil and sauté for another 4 to 5 minutes. Add the white wine, bring to a boil, then cook down to 3 to 4 tablespoons. Return onions to pan, then add sour cream, yogurt, and ginger and remove from heat. Mix well; toss with pasta.

Serves 4

Each serving provides:

671	Calories	107 g	Carbohydrate
23 g	Protein	89 mg	Sodium
16 g	Fat	21 mg	Cholesterol

Sicilian Pizza

PREPARATION TIME: 30 minutes

Some ready-to-bake pizza crusts and focaccia breads are very good and work well for pizza. You can also use a baguette—just slice it in half lengthwise and then into long pieces. Use a good bread and you'll love this pizza.

1	ready-to-bake pizza crust or focaccia bread
1/4	cup olive oil
1	pound eggplant, peeled and cut into small cubes
3	cloves garlic, minced
1/2	cup dry red wine
10	olives
1	teaspoon serrano or other hot pepper, seeded and minced
1/8	teaspoon salt
1/8	teaspoon pepper
1	tablespoon oregano
1	cup grated mozzarella cheese

Preheat oven to 450°. Rub the crust or bread with a little of the olive oil. Heat all but 2 to 3 tablespoons of the remaining olive oil and fry the eggplant and garlic over medium-low heat until the eggplant softens, about 8 minutes. Add the wine, olives, serrano, salt, and pepper and cook 3 to 4 minutes. Spread the filling over the bread and sprinkle with oregano and cheese. Drizzle the remaining olive oil on top. Bake about 15 minutes.

Serves 4

Each serving provides:

440	Calories	44 g	Carbohydrate
14 g	Protein	640 mg	Sodium
22 g	Fat	16 mg	Cholesterol

Spaghetti with Hot Pepper Sauce

<small>PREPARATION TIME:</small> 25 minutes

Turning oil into pepper oil is simple with a jalapeño. If you happen to have hot pepper oil on hand, just use that and forget making your own.

12	ounces spaghetti
7	mushrooms, sliced
1/2	sweet red pepper, seeded and julienned
1/2	cup extra-virgin olive oil
4	cloves garlic, minced
1	jalapeño, seeded and sliced
2	tablespoons fresh parsley, chopped

Cook the spaghetti according to package directions. Meanwhile, sauté the mushroom and sweet pepper in 3 tablespoons of the oil until soft, about 8 minutes. In a separate saucepan, heat the remaining 5 tablespoons of oil with the garlic and hot pepper and cook on medium-low heat for about 8 minutes. Discard the hot pepper, then mix the oil with the mushrooms and sweet peppers. Add this mixture to the pasta and toss with parsley.

Serves 4

Each serving provides:

587	Calories	71 g	Carbohydrate
12 g	Protein	7 mg	Sodium
29 g	Fat	0 mg	Cholesterol

Penne with Broccoli

PREPARATION TIME: 20 minutes

Make sure you don't overcook the broccoli for this dish—you want it to have some crunch. If you like, sauté a little red pepper and toss it with the pasta as well.

12	ounces penne or macaroni
1/4	cup extra-virgin olive oil
1	small onion, cut in half and thinly sliced
3	cloves garlic, minced
1/4	cup pine nuts
1	pound broccoli, chopped
1/8	teaspoon salt
1/4	teaspoon pepper
	Parmesan cheese (optional)

Cook the pasta according to package directions. Sauté the onion and garlic in oil over medium-low heat for 6 to 7 minutes. Add the pine nuts, salt, and pepper. Steam the broccoli until crisp-tender. Toss all with the pasta except cheese. Serve the Parmesan cheese on the side.

Serves 4

Each serving provides:

554	Calories	79 g	Carbohydrate
18 g	Protein	98 mg	Sodium
21 g	Fat	0 mg	Cholesterol

Ziti with Herbs

PREPARATION TIME: 15 minutes

I learned my lesson about hot peppers several years ago. Thinking I had rinsed my hands well enough, I went on about my cooking and happened to rub the corner of my eye a few minutes later. After 15 minutes of dousing my eye with cold water I began to recover. Use gloves with these peppers—they are among the hottest!

1	pound ziti, macaroni, or other pasta
2	Scotch bonnet or other hot pepper, whole (see Pepper Chart, page 8)
6	tablespoons extra-virgin olive oil
4	tablespoons fresh parsley, chopped
1/4	cup fresh basil, chopped or torn into pieces
3	tablespoons fresh thyme and/or rosemary or 1 1/2 teaspoons dried
	Parmesan cheese (optional)

Bring water to boil and add the pasta and the whole peppers. Gently heat the olive oil. When the pasta is just about done, stir the chopped herbs into the olive oil. Drain pasta and discard the peppers. (Caution: If peppers happen to split during cooking, make sure the extremely hot seeds are not in the pasta.) Toss the herbs and oil with the pasta. Top with grated Parmesan cheese if desired.

Serves 4

Each serving provides:

625	Calories	90 g	Carbohydrate
15 g	Protein	5 mg	Sodium
22 g	Fat	0 mg	Cholesterol

Fresh Tomato Fettuccine

PREPARATION TIME: 20 minutes

This pasta dish is a perfect way to add a spicy touch to fresh summer tomatoes. For peeling and seeding the tomatoes see Introduction, page 4.

1	pound fettuccine, cooked
6	ripe tomatoes, peeled, seeded, and chopped
1	cup fresh basil leaves, chopped
1/2	cup fresh parsley, chopped
1/4	cup extra-virgin olive oil
5	cloves garlic, minced
1	tablespoon jalapeño or serrano, seeded and minced

Cook the fettuccine according to package directions. Meanwhile, combine the tomatoes, basil, and parsley in a bowl. Heat the oil over medium-low heat and add the garlic. Sauté until just soft, 3 to 4 minutes, then add pepper and sauté another minute. Add to the tomato mixture, then toss all with the pasta.

Serves 4

Each serving provides:

615	Calories	101 g	Carbohydrate
18 g	Protein	25 mg	Sodium
16 g	Fat	0 mg	Cholesterol

Asian "Pesto" Pasta

PREPARATION TIME: 20 minutes

This flavorful sauce brings the ginger and soy flavors to a traditional Italian pesto sauce.

20	basil leaves
1 1/2	cups fresh cilantro leaves, chopped
2	tablespoons fresh ginger, grated
2	teaspoons tamari or soy sauce
1	tablespoon white wine vinegar
1	teaspoon hot pepper, seeded and minced (see Pepper Chart, page 8)
2	cloves garlic, minced
1/4	cup peanut oil
1/4	cup unsalted peanuts (optional)
1	pound linguine or other pasta, cooked

Combine all ingredients except pasta in blender or food processor and puree. Toss with the pasta.

Serves 4

Each serving provides:

576	Calories	92 g	Carbohydrate
16 g	Protein	188 mg	Sodium
16 g	Fat	0 mg	Cholesterol

6

Main
Dishes

For many people, the idea of vegetarian main dishes conjures up what they're missing instead of what they have. I suppose that's to be expected when the term "meatless" is used. Yet we don't think of ourselves as missing something when we order Bok Choy with Black Mushrooms, Fettuccine Alfredo, or even Macaroni & Cheese in a restaurant. Why then, when cooking at home, do we think that eating vegetarian means "missing" something?

As promised in the introduction to this book, there is no tofu in these entrees. Personally, I think tofu has gotten a bad rap—it is a high protein food which absorbs the flavors around it very well. But the resistance is out there, so for those who are not vegetarian, but want to eat less meat, here you will find comforting signposts of old familiar ingredients as you travel along this new path to healthful eating. These dishes, I believe, will serve you well.

Vegetable Stir-Fry with Ginger Sauce

PREPARATION TIME: 25 minutes

The flavor of this sweet sauce is delightful over vegetables and rice. It seems like it should take longer to make for as good as it tastes. I've listed my favorite mix of vegetables but substitute with what's in season and what you have on hand: carrots, broccoli, etc.

6	tablespoons rice vinegar
5	tablespoons sugar
3/4	cup plus 1 1/2 tablespoons water
1	tablespoon cornstarch
2	tablespoons tamari or soy sauce
1	tablespoon fresh ginger, grated
4	tablespoons vegetable oil
1	red pepper, seeded and julienned
1	onion, cut in half and thinly sliced
2	cloves garlic, minced
8	mushrooms, sliced
2	zucchinis, sliced
5	cups cooked rice

Bring the vinegar, sugar, and 3/4 cup of water to a boil. Reduce heat and simmer 5 minutes. Mix the cornstarch with 1 1/2 tablespoons of water, then stir it into the sauce. Add tamari or soy sauce and cook until thickened, about 5 minutes. Remove from heat and stir in the ginger.

In a skillet, heat the oil over medium-high heat and stir-fry the vegetables until crisp-tender. Cook the pepper and the onion for 2 minutes, then add the garlic, mushrooms, and zucchini for 4 to 5 minutes. Spread the vegetables over the rice. Top with the sauce.

Serves 4

Each serving provides:

571	Calories	99 g	Carbohydrate
10 g	Protein	516 mg	Sodium
15 g	Fat	0 mg	Cholesterol

Chile and Sour Cream Quesadillas

PREPARATION TIME: 20 minutes

These fast and spicy quesadillas take just minutes. Start some rice to accompany the entree when you begin working on the quesadillas and everything will be ready at once. To give the rice a little color and complementary flavor, stir in a tablespoon or so of fresh, chopped cilantro.

2	tablespoons butter
3	tablespoons olive or vegetable oil
8	flour tortillas
2	cups grated jack or cheddar cheese
1	to 2 tablespoons jalapeño or serrano, seeded and finely chopped
1/2	mild red or green bell pepper, seeded and finely chopped
	Sour cream
	Salsa (optional)

Melt half of the butter with half of the oil in a large skillet over medium heat. Cover one side of a tortilla with cheese, then sprinkle the chopped peppers on top and cover with a second tortilla. Fry the tortillas in the butter and oil until slightly

browned, then flip and brown the other side. Dry on paper towels and keep warm in the oven while preparing the remaining
quesadillas. Add additional butter and oil as needed. Serve
with sour cream and/or salsa.

Serves 4

Each serving provides:

791	Calories	64 g	Carbohydrate
27 g	Protein	496 mg	Sodium
45 g	Fat	72 mg	Cholesterol

Sweet & Sour & Spicy

Without the jalapeño this dish is pretty close to a sweet & sour stir-fry. The hot pepper gives it a spicy boost. Serve over rice.

1/4	cup catsup
1/8	cup soy sauce
1/3	cup cider vinegar
1/3	cup brown sugar
1/2	cup water
2	tablespoons cornstarch dissolved in 2 tablespoons of water
4	tablespoons vegetable oil
1	small onion, cut in half and thinly sliced
2	cloves garlic, minced
1	jalapeño or serrano, seeded and finely chopped
1	red bell pepper, seeded and julienned
1	green bell pepper, seeded and julienned
1	small zucchini, diced
3	mushrooms, sliced

Mix the first 6 ingredients together in a small saucepan to make the sweet & sour sauce warm. In a skillet, heat the vegetable oil and sauté onion for 3 to 4 minutes, then add garlic and peppers and stir-fry another 3 to 4 minutes. Add zucchini and mushrooms and stir-fry until mushrooms begin to color. Add the sauce and stir another minute. Remove from heat and serve.

Serves 4

Each serving provides:

275	Calories	37 g	Carbohydrate
2 g	Protein	706 mg	Sodium
14 g	Fat	0 mg	Cholesterol

Vegetarian Burritos

PREPARATION TIME: 30 minutes

We enjoy a variety of vegetarian burritos since tortillas lend themselves to many creations. This one is a favorite—you won't miss the meat.

3	tablespoons vegetable oil
1	onion, finely chopped
1	red or green bell pepper, seeded and finely chopped
1	jalapeño, seeded and finely chopped
1	teaspoon ground cumin
2	cloves garlic, minced
1	cup black beans, canned okay (see Introduction)
1	small zucchini, diced
6	to 8 flour tortillas
	Cheddar or jack cheese
	Shredded iceberg lettuce
	Sour cream
	Salsa

Sauté the onion and peppers in oil until soft, about 7 minutes. Add the cumin, garlic, black beans, and zucchini and sauté for about 6 minutes more, until the zucchini is cooked but still crisp. Heat the tortillas in a dry skillet until just warm, or place in a microwave, cover loosely with a paper towel and heat for 40 seconds. Place filling in each tortilla, top with sprinkled cheese and place under the broiler until the cheese melts. Sprinkle with shredded lettuce and serve with salsa and sour cream.

Serves 4

Each serving provides:

636	Calories	69 g	Carbohydrate
23 g	Protein	637 mg	Sodium
29 g	Fat	30 mg	Cholesterol

Three-Pepper Chili

PREPARATION TIME: 20 minutes (plus 25 minutes cooking time)

A nice, warming mixture of beans and peppers, this is a spicy chili you'll want to serve with cornbread on the side.

1	tablespoon olive oil
1	cup red bell pepper, seeded and chopped
1/2	cup Anaheim or other mild pepper, seeded and chopped
2	tablespoons jalapeño, seeded and minced
1/2	cup onion, chopped
3	cloves garlic, minced
1	tablespoon ground cumin
1	tablespoon chili powder
2	teaspoons paprika
1/2	cup pineapple juice
1	28-ounce can Italian-style plum tomatoes with juice, chopped
1	15-ounce can red kidney beans, rinsed and drained
1	15-ounce can white kidney beans (cannellini beans), rinsed and drained
1	15-ounce can black beans, rinsed and drained

Heat the olive oil and sauté the peppers, onion, and garlic over low heat until soft, about 8 minutes. Stir in the spices, then add the remaining ingredients and bring to a boil. Simmer 25 minutes, adding water if needed.

Serves 6

Each serving provides:

241	Calories	43 g	Carbohydrate
12 g	Protein	735 mg	Sodium
4 g	Fat	0 mg	Cholesterol

Spicy Shish Kabobs

PREPARATION TIME: 30 minutes

Why should shish kabobs be limited to the carnivores? Shi-itake mushrooms, if available, are meatier than other mush-rooms and hold up to barbecuing a little better.

2	tablespoons olive oil
1/2	onion, finely chopped
1/2	sweet pepper, seeded and finely chopped
1	stalk celery, finely chopped
2	cloves garlic, minced
1/4	teaspoon paprika
1/2	teaspoon ground coriander
1/8	teaspoon cayenne pepper
1/8	teaspoon chili powder
1/2	teaspoon dried basil
1	teaspoon fresh thyme or 1/2 teaspoon dried
1/8	teaspoon pepper
1/2	cup vegetable broth or water
1/2	cup tomato sauce
1/8	teaspoon Tabasco or other hot sauce
3	zucchinis, cut into 1/2-inch slices
1	pound cherry tomatoes
8	to 10 mushrooms (shiitake, crimini, or button)
4	sweet peppers, seeded and cut into squares

Heat the oil in a skillet, then add onion, chopped pepper, celery, and garlic. Add the seasonings and mix well. Sauté over medium-low heat, stirring occasionally, until onion and peppers are soft, about 8 minutes. Add broth or water, tomato sauce, and Tabasco, increase to a boil, then simmer uncovered until sauce thickens, about 15 minutes. Preheat a charcoal fire or broiler and thread the vegetables onto a skewer. Brush them with the sauce so that all sides are well coated. If broiling, place in a dish and broil for about 5 minutes, turning frequently. If grilling, place over medium-hot coals and grill about 5 minutes on each side.

Serves 4

Each serving provides:

154	Calories	21 g	Carbohydrate
4 g	Protein	217 mg	Sodium
8 g	Fat	0 mg	Cholesterol

Mushroom and Cilantro Tostadas

PREPARATION TIME: 30 minutes

Tostadas are frequently my answer to a quick dinner. I like the crunch of the tortilla with a variety of toppings.

1/4	cup vegetable oil
6	corn tortillas
1/4	cup onion, finely diced
2	tablespoons jalapeño, seeded and finely diced
1/4	cup red or green bell pepper, seeded and finely diced
2	cloves garlic, minced
1	pound mushrooms (crimini or button), sliced
3	tablespoons fresh cilantro, finely chopped
	Salsa
	Sour cream (optional)

In a skillet, heat the vegetable oil until hot, then add tortillas one at a time. Fry the tortillas, turning once, until crisp, about a minute on each side. Drain on paper towels and set aside. Rinse the skillet of all but 3 tablespoons of oil, and sauté the onion and peppers until just soft, about 5 minutes. Add the garlic and sauté another minute. Add mushrooms and cilantro and cook until mushrooms have softened, about 7 minutes. Scoop the mushroom mixture onto the tortilla and serve with salsa and sour cream, if desired, on top.

Makes 6 tostadas

Each tostada provides:

186	Calories	22 g	Carbohydrate
4 g	Protein	219 mg	Sodium
10 g	Fat	0 mg	Cholesterol

Mexican Stuffed Peppers

PREPARATION TIME: 35 minutes (plus 30 minutes baking time)

Stuffed, sweet peppers with a spicy filling makes a great dinner. Try a salad with a cilantro-infused vinaigrette on the side.

1	tablespoon vegetable or olive oil
1	onion, chopped
1	jalapeño, seeded and minced
2	cloves garlic, minced
1	tablespoon good-quality chili powder
1/2	teaspoon cumin
1 1/4	cups rice
1	15-ounce can tomatoes, with juice
2	cups vegetable broth, or water
4	red or green bell peppers, cored and seeded
	Parmesan or cheddar cheese (optional)

Preheat oven to 350°. Sauté the onion and jalapeño in oil until soft, then add garlic, chili powder, and cumin. Stir in rice and cook, stirring, until golden, 4 to 5 minutes. Add the tomatoes and broth or water, bring to a boil, then cover and reduce heat. Simmer 25 minutes.

Meanwhile, blanch the peppers in boiling water for 5 minutes and drain. Place peppers in a baking dish. Spoon rice mixture into peppers. Place the baking dish into another pan with 1/2 inch of water, cover lightly with foil and bake 30 minutes. If desired, grate Parmesan or cheddar cheese on top and cook uncovered for an additional 5 minutes or until lightly browned.

Serves 4

Each serving provides:

324	Calories	64 g	Carbohydrate
7 g	Protein	210 mg	Sodium
5 g	Fat	0 mg	Cholesterol

Fiery Zucchini Casserole

PREPARATION TIME: 25 minutes

This quick casserole is strictly a stovetop dish, and it is a complete meal. To cool it off, cut down on the red pepper flakes.

2 tablespoons vegetable or olive oil
1 onion, chopped
4 zucchinis, thinly sliced
1 clove garlic, minced
2 medium tomatoes, peeled, with juice (or 1 14-ounce can with juice)
1/2 teaspoon red pepper flakes
1/8 teaspoon ground cayenne
1 1/2 cups cooked rice

Sauté the onion in oil until soft, about 5 minutes. Add zucchini and sauté another 3 to 4 minutes. Add remaining ingredients, cover, and simmer about 15 minutes.

Serves 4

Each serving provides:

220	Calories	34 g	Carbohydrate
5 g	Protein	10 mg	Sodium
8 g	Fat	0 mg	Cholesterol

Vegetable-Pepper Casserole

PREPARATION TIME: 15 minutes (plus 25 minutes baking time)

This is a quick casserole supper with a warm mix of vegetables and spices.

1   tablespoon olive oil
1   onion, chopped
1   serrano, seeded and minced
2   cloves garlic, minced
2¹/₂ cups cooked rice
2   zucchinis, shredded
2   tomatoes, peeled and chopped
¹/₄ cup Parmesan cheese, freshly grated
2   tablespoons vegetable broth or water
2   teaspoons fresh oregano or 1 teaspoon dried

Preheat oven to 350°. Sauté the onion, pepper, and garlic in the oil over low heat until soft, then combine with remaining ingredients in a baking dish and bake for 25 minutes.

Serves 4

~~~~~~~~~~~~~~~~~~

Each serving provides:

274	Calories	48 g	Carbohydrate
8 g	Protein	104 mg	Sodium
6 g	Fat	4 mg	Cholesterol

Black Bean One-Skillet Casserole

PREPARATION TIME: 35 minutes

The black beans really aren't the star here—the spices and serrano are. And since this is not "pan-intensive," clean-up is a snap.

1	tablespoon olive oil
1	onion, chopped
1	large carrot, finely chopped
1	serrano, seeded and minced
3	cloves garlic, minced
2	cups black beans (see Introduction, page 3)
1/4	cup vegetable broth or water
2	tablespoons ground coriander
1/2	teaspoon dried marjoram
1/2	cup cheddar cheese, grated

Preheat oven to 350°. Heat oil and sauté the onion, carrots, pepper, and garlic for 4 to 5 minutes. Add remaining ingredients except the cheese, and sauté for another 1 to 2 minutes. Bake 10 minutes, then cover with cheese, and bake another 5 to 10 minutes.

Serves 4

Each serving provides:

240	Calories	31 g	Carbohydrate
12 g	Protein	561 mg	Sodium
9 g	Fat	14 mg	Cholesterol

Mex-Italian Frittata

PREPARATION TIME: 35 minutes (includes making the sauce)

This zucchini frittata, a la Italy, is covered with a green sauce common in Mexican foods. In fact, you can use any extra sauce for enchiladas the next night.

4   medium zucchinis, cubed
2   tablespoons olive oil
1   teaspoon jalapeño, seeded and minced
6   large eggs
1/4 cup Monterey Jack cheese
     Mexican Green Sauce (page 26)

Sauté the zucchini in 1 tablespoon olive oil for about 10 minutes, add the pepper to the skillet, sauté for a minute or two longer, then remove from heat.

Beat the eggs and mix with the cheese. Add zucchini mixture to the eggs and stir. Heat the second tablespoon of olive oil in the pan over medium heat and pour the egg mixture in. Reduce heat to low and cook slowly until almost set in the middle. Remove and turn (or place under a broiler to finish cooking the other side). Pour green sauce over the frittata and serve.

Serves 4

Each serving not including Green Sauce provides:

218	Calories	5 g	Carbohydrate
13 g	Protein	136 mg	Sodium
17 g	Fat	326 mg	Cholesterol

Colorful Couscous Casserole

PREPARATION TIME: 20 minutes (plus 25 minutes baking time)

As pretty on the plate as it is delightful on the palate, this dish has a nice, spicy bite. You can serve a little Harissa (page 18) on the side if you wish.

1	tablespoon vegetable oil
1/2	onion, chopped
1/2	bell pepper, seeded and chopped
2	tablespoons jalapeño or serrano, seeded and minced
1 1/2	cups water
1	cup couscous, uncooked
2	cups black beans, drained (see Introduction, page 3)
1/4	cup sliced water chestnuts
1	cup lowfat ricotta cheese
2	tablespoons rice vinegar
2	teaspoons peanut oil
1/4	teaspoon cayenne pepper

Preheat oven to 350°. Heat oil in a skillet and sauté the onion and peppers until soft, about 5 minutes. Heat water to a boil, remove from heat, and stir in the couscous. Cover and let stand until couscous is tender and water absorbed, about 5 minutes. Stir in black beans, onion, peppers, and water chestnuts. In a separate bowl, combine remaining ingredients then stir into the couscous mixture. Lightly coat a baking dish with oil or butter, spoon in the mixture, and bake, uncovered, for 25 minutes.

Serves 4

Each serving provides:

439	Calories	63 g	Carbohydrate
21 g	Protein	547 mg	Sodium
12 g	Fat	19 mg	Cholesterol

Andrew's Mushroom Ta-Rito

PREPARATION TIME: 20 minutes

My teenager Andrew is a big fan of these. I don't know if this qualifies as a taco or a burrito, so I just call it a ta-rito. Serve with rice or beans or both.

3	tablespoons vegetable oil
1	onion, chopped
2	cloves garlic, minced
1	pound mushrooms, thinly sliced
2	jalapeños, seeded and minced
1	small can tomatoes (14-oz. can), drained and chopped, or 3/4 pound fresh
2	tablespoons fresh cilantro, chopped
1/4	pound jack or cheddar cheese, grated
6	flour tortillas
	Fresh salsa (optional)

Heat oil in a skillet and add onion and garlic. Sauté for 2 to 3 minutes, then add the mushrooms and peppers. Sauté another 3 to 4 minutes, add tomatoes, and sauté 10 minutes. Remove from heat and stir in the cilantro and cheese. Heat the tortillas in a dry skillet or microwave, then spoon in the filling, fold over, and top with salsa.

Makes 6 ta-ritos

Each ta-rito serving provides:

326	Calories	40 g	Carbohydrate
10 g	Protein	107 mg	Sodium
14 g	Fat	5 mg	Cholesterol

Hot & Spicy Fried Rice

PREPARATION TIME: 25 minutes

This quick rice dish goes well with a variety of foods, or is a complete and colorful dinner on its own.

4	cups cooked rice, cold
5	tablespoons peanut or corn oil
1	onion, diced
1¹/₂	small red bell peppers, seeded and diced
1	carrot, diced
¹/₄	teaspoon dried red pepper flakes
3	scallions, thinly sliced

Separate the chilled rice with a fork. Heat a skillet or wok over medium-high heat until hot, add the oil and swirl to coat the pan. Add the onion and toss until hot, about 2 minutes. Reduce heat to medium, add the pepper and carrot, and toss for another 2 to 3 minutes. Stir in the rice and red pepper flakes. Remove from heat and stir in the scallions.

Serves 4

Each serving provides:

456	Calories	67 g	Carbohydrate
7 g	Protein	15 mg	Sodium
18 g	Fat	0 mg	Cholesterol

Mexican "Quiche"

PREPARATION TIME: 20 minutes (plus 25 minutes baking time)

Perfect with a salad, or try it with Quick Mexican Vegetables (page 89).

4	corn tortillas
	Vegetable oil
3	tablespoons flour
$1/2$	teaspoon good-quality chili powder
$1/8$	teaspoon salt
1	medium tomato, chopped
2	tablespoons jalapeño, seeded and minced
4	to 5 green onions, sliced
$1/3$	cup salsa
3	eggs, beaten
$1/2$	cup milk
$1/2$	cup jack or cheddar cheese, grated

Preheat oven to 350°. Warm the tortillas in a dry skillet until soft, then coat an 11- × 8- × 2-inch baking dish with the oil and arrange the tortillas to cover. In a bowl, combine the flour, chili powder, and salt. Sprinkle the tortillas with a little of the flour mixture. Top with the tomato, pepper, and onion. Sprinkle again with the flour mixture. Spoon salsa over the top. Combine the eggs and milk well and pour over the vegetables. Bake, uncovered, about 20 to 25 minutes or until a toothpick inserted comes out clean. Top with cheese and bake until cheese melts.

Serves 4

Each serving provides:

239	Calories	25 g	Carbohydrate
12 g	Protein	368 mg	Sodium
10 g	Fat	175 mg	Cholesterol

Curried Vegetables

This works as a main dish—just serve over the rice you made while the vegetables simmered.

1	tablespoon vegetable oil
1	small onion, chopped
3	cloves garlic, minced
1/4	teaspoon cayenne
1/2	teaspoon ground cumin
1	tablespoon ground coriander
2	teaspoons ground cardamom
1/2	teaspoon turmeric
1/2	teaspoon cinnamon
1 1/2	teaspoons freshly grated ginger
1/4	teaspoon salt
2	cups cauliflower florets
2	carrots, sliced
2	zucchinis, sliced
1/2	pound fresh green beans, trimmed and cut into 1-inch pieces
2	cups vegetable broth
	Cooked rice

Heat a pot with the oil over medium heat. Add the onion and cook until soft, about 5 minutes. Add garlic and the next 8 ingredients and stir constantly for about 1 minute, being careful not to burn the garlic. Add the vegetables and stir well to mix. Cover, reduce heat, and simmer about 20 minutes until the vegetables are tender. Serve over rice.

Serves 4

Each serving not including rice provides:

131	Calories	21 g	Carbohydrate
5 g	Protein	162 mg	Sodium
4 g	Fat	0 mg	Cholesterol

Pepper and Bean Enchiladas with Green Sauce

PREPARATION TIME: 35 minute (plus 15 minutes baking time, includes making the sauce)

Enchiladas with this green sauce are a snap to make, and a filling dinner.

	Mexican Green Sauce (see page 26)
2	tablespoons vegetable oil
2	teaspoons ground cumin
1	tablespoon ground coriander
1	sweet red pepper, julienned
2	cups black beans, canned okay (see Introduction)
16	fresh corn tortillas
1	small onion, chopped
1/2	cup cheddar cheese (optional)

While the sauce is cooking, add the oil to a separate saucepan and stir in cumin and coriander. Add the pepper and sauté for about 5 minutes. Add beans to the pan, mix well, and cook until warm.

Pour the finished sauce onto a plate and dip the tortillas in the sauce. Spoon 2 tablespoons of bean-pepper mixture along with a teaspoon of the onion into the tortillas. Add cheese if desired. Fold over and pin with a toothpick. Repeat, placing all of the tortillas in baking dishes. Pour remaining sauce over and bake until bubbly, about 15 minutes.

Serves 8

Each serving not including sauce provides:

230	Calories	39 g	Carbohydrate
7 g	Protein	340 mg	Sodium
5 g	Fat	0 mg	Cholesterol

Grilled Vegetables with Ginger Barbecue Sauce

PREPARATION TIME: 30 minutes (plus 25 minutes simmer time)

The non-vegetarians in your house will want to try this barbecue sauce with meat. It's also great with vegetables and matches perfectly the smoky flavor of summer barbecue.

2	tablespoons vegetable oil
2	medium onions, chopped
5	cloves garlic, chopped
1	2-inch piece of ginger, sliced
2	cups tomato sauce
2	tablespoons Dijon mustard
1/3	cup vinegar
1	cup water
1	bay leaf
4	tablespoons Worcestershire sauce
2	tablespoons brown sugar
2	tablespoons molasses
1/2	teaspoon cayenne
1/4	teaspoon salt
3	eggplants, peeled, sliced, and grilled 6 to 7 minutes per side
3	sweet peppers, peeled, seeded, sliced into thick strips, brushed with olive oil, and grilled until just blackened, about 4 minutes per side
2	zucchinis, sliced, grilled about 4 minutes per side
	Cooked rice

Sauté the onion in the oil for 3 to 4 minutes, then add garlic and sauté until soft, another 3 minutes. Place in a blender or food processor with the ginger and puree. Return to the skillet with the remaining ingredients except grilled vegetables and rice, and bring to a boil. Reduce heat and simmer about 25 minutes, stirring occasionally. Place vegetables on rice and pour sauce on top.

Serves 4

Each serving not including rice provides:

357	Calories	67 g	Carbohydrate
8 g	Protein	1250 mg	Sodium
10 g	Fat	0 mg	Cholesterol

Zucchini Stuffed with Herbs and Cheese

PREPARATION TIME: 25 minutes (plus 25 minutes baking time)

These stuffed zucchinis go nicely with a green salad, which can be fixed while this bakes.

6	medium zucchinis, whole
2	tablespoons olive oil
3	cloves garlic, minced
1	cup mushrooms, chopped
1/2	teaspoon fresh dill or 1/4 teaspoon dried
1/2	teaspoon fresh thyme or 1/4 teaspoon dried
1/2	teaspoon fresh marjoram or 1/4 teaspoon dried
2/3	cup white wine
1	cup bread crumbs
11/4	cups Parmesan cheese, grated

Preheat oven to 350°. Steam the zucchinis whole for 5 minutes, until just softening. Trim the ends and cut in half lengthwise. Scoop out the center, making a hollow for the stuffing.

Sauté the garlic, mushrooms, and herbs in the oil over medium-low heat for about 10 minutes. Add the white wine, increase heat to high, and cook 4 minutes or until the wine is reduced by half. Remove the mushroom mixture to a separate bowl and combine with the bread crumbs and $1/2$ cup of the Parmesan. Place the mixture into the zucchini halves and top with the remaining Parmesan. Bake in an oiled baking dish for 25 minutes, until brown.

Serves 4

Each serving provides:

329	Calories	27 g	Carbohydrate
16 g	Protein	659 mg	Sodium
16 g	Fat	21 mg	Cholesterol

Cheese, Tomato, and Hot Pepper Sandwiches

PREPARATION TIME: 15 minutes (plus 20 minutes soaking time)

This pepper paste works nicely on these sandwiches and others as well.

2	jalapeños, seeded and coarsley chopped
6	tablespoons vegetable oil
4	slices bread
	Soft butter
3	slices cheddar cheese
1	tomato, sliced
1/2	small, sweet onion, sliced

Pour boiling water over the peppers to cover and let sit for 15 to 20 minutes, until softened, then drain. Combine with the oil in a food processor, or chop finely and use a mortar and pestle to make a paste. Spread the jalapeño paste on one side of each piece of bread. Butter the other side then add the cheddar, tomato, and onion, top with the other slice of bread and grill over medium heat, using a cover to help the cheese melt.

Makes 2 sandwiches

Each sandwich provides:

736	Calories	33 g	Carbohydrate
17 g	Protein	499 mg	Sodium
62 g	Fat	51 mg	Cholesterol

Spicy Eggplant Casserole

PREPARATION TIME: 30 minutes

With simple and direct flavors, this filling dish is great preceded by a bean salad.

5   small eggplants, peeled and thinly sliced
6   tablespoons olive oil
4   ripe tomatoes, peeled, seeded, and diced
1   onion, cut in half and thinly sliced
3   cloves garlic, minced
1/2 teaspoon red pepper flakes

In a large skillet, sauté just enough eggplant slices to cover the bottom of the pan, until golden. Repeat with other slices. Combine all ingredients and cook over low heat until all the vegetables are tender, 15 to 20 minutes.

Serves 4

Each serving provides:

365	Calories	43 g	Carbohydrate
6 g	Protein	27 mg	Sodium
22 g	Fat	0 mg	Cholesterol

Four-Alarm Stir-Fry

PREPARATION TIME: 25 minutes

This stir-fry is for those who enjoy very hot foods. The key is to keep stirring—have everything chopped or grated and ready to add before you begin. As with most stir-fries this is a complete meal all by itself.

1	teaspoon cornstarch dissolved in 1/4 cup vegetable broth or water
1	tablespoon soy sauce
1	teaspoon sesame oil
1/2	teaspoon crushed red pepper flakes
2	teaspoons honey
5	tablespoons vegetable oil
2	carrots, peeled and sliced
10	mushrooms, quartered
1	sweet onion, cut in half and thinly sliced
1	clove garlic, minced
1	inch fresh ginger, grated or minced
1	sweet red or green pepper, seeded and diced
2	tablespoons jalapeño, seeded and finely chopped
	Cooked rice

Combine the cornstarch and broth with the soy sauce, sesame oil, red pepper flakes, and honey to make the sauce. In a skillet or wok, heat the oil over high heat and add the carrots and mushrooms, stirring constantly for about 5 minutes. Add onion and stir another minute, then garlic and ginger and stir another minute, being careful not to let the garlic burn. Add peppers and cook another 2 minutes. Pour in sauce and bring to a boil, stirring constantly. Remove from heat and spoon over rice.

Serves 4

Each serving not including rice provides:

240	Calories	17 g	Carbohydrate
2 g	Protein	280 mg	Sodium
19 g	Fat	0 mg	Cholesterol

Black Bean and Jicama Tostadas

Preparation Time: 20 minutes (includes making salsa)

This delicious salsa practically makes a meal in itself. If you choose, you can opt to top with cheese, sour cream, or even tomato salsa.

	Black Bean Salsa (see page 18)
1/4	cup vegetable oil
6	corn tortillas
	Jack or cheddar cheese, grated (optional)
	Sour cream (optional)

Make the salsa as directed. Mix well. In a skillet, heat the vegetable oil until hot, then add the tortillas one at a time. Fry the tortillas, turning once, until crisp, up to a minute on each side. Drain on paper towels, top with the salsa or topping of your choice, and serve.

Makes 6 tostadas

Each tostada provides:

234	Calories	29 g	Carbohydrate
7 g	Protein	402 mg	Sodium
10 g	Fat	0 mg	Cholesterol

Potatoes and Rice with Spice

PREPARATION TIME: 20 minutes (plus 25 minutes cooking time)

The rice and potatoes soak up the spices in this stovetop casserole.

4	tablespoons vegetable oil
1	onion, chopped
1/2	teaspoon ground cumin
1	clove garlic, minced
1	potato, diced
1/4	teaspoon ground cayenne
1/4	teaspoon oregano
3	cups rice
4	cups vegetable broth, or water

Heat oil in a large pot over medium heat. Add the onion and stir until soft, about 7 minutes. Add cumin, garlic, and the potato. Fry until potato begins to brown. Add cayenne, oregano, and rice and stir 3 to 4 minutes. Add vegetable broth, bring to a boil, and cover. Reduce heat to low and simmer 25 minutes or until all of the moisture is absorbed.

Serves 6

Each serving provides:

475	Calories	86 g	Carbohydrate
8 g	Protein	9 mg	Sodium
10 g	Fat	0 mg	Cholesterol

Fruit Curry over Rice

PREPARATION TIME: 30 minutes

This sweet dish makes a delightful dinner. I use frozen fruit which makes it quick and easy as well. Feel free to substitute fruit you have on hand, such as grapes or pears. Serve a vegetable or cucumber salad on the side.

2	tablespoons olive oil
1/8	teaspoon cayenne
1/4	teaspoon ground cumin
1	teaspoon *each* ground cardamom and coriander
1/2	teaspoon turmeric
1	teaspon paprika
1/4	teaspoon cinnamon
1/8	teaspoon salt
1 1/2	tablespoons fresh ginger, grated
5	tablespoons vegetable broth
1	cup fresh or frozen peaches, peeled and chopped
1	cup fresh or frozen plums, peeled and chopped
1/4	cup pineapple, minced
2	tablespoons brown sugar
	Cooked rice

Heat the oil over low heat and add spices. Stir 3 to 4 minutes, add vegetable broth, and increase heat to a boil. Reduce broth by about a third, then add fruit and brown sugar. Cook until syrupy, about 20 minutes. Pour over rice (or over grilled vegetables).

Serves 4

Each serving not including rice provides:

158	Calories	24 g	Carbohydrate
1 g	Protein	72 mg	Sodium
8 g	Fat	0 mg	Cholesterol

Baked Zucchini with Pepper Sauce

PREPARATION TIME: 25 minutes

I use roasted red peppers from jars when I'm in a hurry, although they don't offer the flavor of freshly roasted peppers. To roast your own, see page 4. A good dish with rice.

4	tablespoons olive oil
4	roasted red peppers, seeded and chopped
1	tablespoon jalapeño, seeded and minced
1/2	teaspoon dried oregano
1/8	teaspoon salt
1/4	teaspoon pepper
6	zucchinis
	Parmesan cheese (optional)

Preheat oven to 375°. Sauté the peppers, oregano, salt, and pepper in olive oil for 3 to 4 minutes, then remove to a blender or food processor and puree. Blanch the zucchini in boiling water for about 3 minutes. Remove and rinse under cold water. Trim and cut each zucchini lengthwise, then scoop out seeds.

Place zucchini in an oiled baking dish, rub with a little olive oil, and bake 6 minutes. Spoon sauce into zucchini and bake another 12 minutes. Top with Parmesan, if desired, for the last 2 to 3 minutes of baking time.

Serves 4

Each serving provides:

169	Calories	11 g	Carbohydrate
3 g	Protein	72 mg	Sodium
14 g	Fat	0 mg	Cholesterol

Vegetables in Raw Tomato Sauce

PREPARATION TIME: 30 minutes (plus standing time—recommended for best flavor—of 90 minutes)

This Provençal sauce is traditionally served with fish but I find the style goes well with sautéed and raw vegetables. With all these fresh ingredients I like to use fresh herbs, although dried thyme does pretty well. Top with a little cheese if you like.

3/4 cup extra-virgin olive oil
8 medium, ripe tomatoes, peeled, seeded, and chopped
2 tablespoons red wine vinegar
5 niçoise or calamata olives, pitted and finely chopped
3 cloves garlic, finely chopped or minced
1/8 teaspoon salt
1/4 teaspoon pepper
2 medium zucchinis, trimmed and sliced
3 carrots, trimmed and sliced
1 head broccoli florets, chopped
1 tablespoon fresh parsley, chopped
2 teaspoons fresh rosemary, chopped
2 teaspoons fresh thyme, chopped, or 1 teaspoon dried
2 teaspoons chives or scallions, chopped

Combine 1/2 cup of the oil, the tomatoes, vinegar, olives, garlic, salt, and pepper in a bowl and let sit for 90 minutes or more for flavors to blend. Briefly steam the carrots to soften slightly, about 3 minutes. Heat the remaining 1/4 cup of oil in a skillet and add the zucchini, carrots, and broccoli. Cook until just crisp-tender, about 7 to 10 minutes. Stir the herbs into the sauce. Serve the vegetables with the tomato sauce spooned on top.

Serves 4

Each serving provides:

483	Calories	25 g	Carbohydrate
6 g	Protein	220 mg	Sodium
43 g	Fat	0 mg	Cholesterol

Pineapple Stir-Fried Rice

PREPARATION TIME: 25 minutes

Cold rice is the key to successful stir-fried rice. This is perfect for leftover rice, or make rice in the morning and leave it in the refrigerator all day so it will be ready to stir-fry when you get home.

1/4	cup sesame or peanut oil
1	3-inch piece of fresh ginger, grated
1	jalapeño, seeded and minced
1	clove garlic, minced
4	tablespoons lemon zest
3	cups cooked cold rice
1	cup pineapple, finely chopped
1	cup fresh cilantro, finely chopped

Heat a skillet or wok over medium high heat then add the oil, ginger, pepper, and garlic and stir-fry 1 minute, being careful not to burn the ginger or garlic. Add the lemon zest and rice and stir until heated. Stir in the pineapple and cilantro until heated.

Serves 4

Each serving provides:

393	Calories	62 g	Carbohydrate
5 g	Protein	17 mg	Sodium
14 g	Fat	0 mg	Cholesterol

Sweet & Sour Cabbage

PREPARATION TIME: 25 minutes

The cabbage really soaks up the sweet & sour flavors.

1   tablespoon peanut oil
1   small onion, cut in half and thinly sliced
2   carrots, thinly sliced
1/2 head green cabbage, chopped
1/3 cup honey
1/3 cup cider vinegar
1   teaspoon fresh ginger, grated
2   teaspoons cornstarch
1   teaspoon soy sauce
     Cooked rice

Sauté the onion and carrot in the oil over medium-high heat, stirring to keep the onion from burning. Add cabbage and continue cooking for 3 minutes. Add 1/4 cup of water, cover, reduce heat, and cook for 10 minutes. Combine remaining ingredients, except the rice, stirring the cornstarch to dissolve. Add to the vegetables and stir until sauce thickens. Serve over rice.

Serves 4

Each serving provides:

184	Calories	39 g	Carbohydrate
3 g	Protein	121 mg	Sodium
4 g	Fat	0 mg	Cholesterol

Vegetables in Spanish Rice

PREPARATION TIME: 40 minutes (plus 20 minutes cooking time)

This dish takes longer than any other in the book to prepare, but it's worth it. It's a complete meal with vegetables, starches—and a little spice.

1/4	cup extra-virgin olive oil
3	cloves garlic, minced
1	onion, minced
1	sweet pepper, seeded and diced
1/2	teaspoon cayenne
1/8	teaspoon salt
1/4	teaspoon pepper
1/2	pound red or Yukon gold potatoes, diced
1/2	cup canned tomatoes, drained
5	cups vegetable broth or water
1	pound fresh green beans, trimmed and cut in 1-inch pieces
1	16-ounce can red kidney beans, drained
1	pound fresh asparagus, cut in 1-inch pieces
1	pound fresh peas, thawed if frozen
2	cups rice

In a large pot, sauté the garlic, onion, and pepper in the oil until soft, about 10 minutes. Add spices, potatoes, and tomatoes and continue to sauté for another 10 minutes. Add the broth and bring to a boil, then add beans. Reduce heat, cover, and cook for 5 minutes, then add remaining ingredients, return to a boil, reduce heat, and cover, cooking 20 to 25 more minutes, or until rice is done.

Serves 6

Each serving provides:

521	Calories	92 g	Carbohydrate
16 g	Protein	310 mg	Sodium
11 g	Fat	0 mg	Cholesterol

Index

A
Almonds in Curried Waldorf Salad, 32
Anaheim chiles, 8
Three-Pepper Chili, 140–141
Ancho chiles, 8
Andrew's Mushroom Ta–Rito, 154
Apples
Curried Apple Coleslaw, 43
Waldorf Salad, Curried, 32
Watercress, Gorgonzola, and Pear Salad, 40–41
Asian "Pesto" Pasta, 129
Asparagus
with Ginger-Lemon Dressing, 83
Spaghetti Verdura, 119
Spanish Rice, Vegetables in, 180–181
Avocados
Soup, 79
Spicy Avocado Salsa, 20

B
Baked Zucchini with Pepper Sauce, 174–175
Balsamic vinegar, 2
Banana peppers, 8
Basil, 7
Asian "Pesto" Pasta, 129
-Cilantro Pesto, 57
Fresh Tomato Fettuccine, 128
Hot Pesto, 24
Lemon Spaghetti, 112
Ziti with Herbs, 126–127
Zucchini-Basil Soup, 68–69
Bay leaf, 7
Beans, 3–4. See also specific beans
Bean Salad with Orange Vinaigrette, 56

Bell peppers, 8
Baked Zucchini with Pepper Sauce, 174–175
Black Bean
and Pepper Salad, 35
Vegetable Salad, 50
Burritos, Vegetarian, 138–139
Chickpea and Pasta Salad, Spicy, 54–55
Chile and Sour Cream Quesadillas, 134–135
Cold Tomato and Roasted Pepper Soup, 76
Corn Salad, Spicy, 53
Couscous Casserole, Colorful, 152–153
Fettuccine with Peas and Peppers, 118
Four-Alarm Stir-Fry, 168–169
Fried Rice, Hot & Spicy, 155
Gazpacho, 75
Greens and Beans, Spicy, 90
Grilled Vegetables with Ginger Barbecue Sauce, 162–163
Jicama Slaw with Cilantro Vinaigrette, 47
Mediterranean Rice, 95
Mexican Stuffed Peppers, 146–147
Mexican Vegetables, Quick, 89
Mushroom and Cilantro Tostadas, 144–145
Penne with Peppers, 116
Pepper and Bean Enchiladas with Green Sauce, 160–161
Pepperpot Soup, 60–61
Pineapple Salsa, 22
Potato-Jicama Salad, 44–45
Ratatouille Pizza, 114–115
Red Pepper Soup, 71

Rice
   and Black Bean Salad,
     48–49
   with Cheese, 92
   and Raisins, Hot, Spicy,
     84–85
   Shish Kabobs, Spicy, 142–143
   Slaw, Sweet & Spicy, 34
   Spaghetti with Hot Pepper
     Sauce, 124
   Spanish Rice, 98
   Spicy Peach Salsa, 21
   Stuffed with Pasta and Cheese,
     120–121
   Sweet & Sour & Spicy, 136–137
   Teriyaki Mushrooms and
     Peppers, 100
   Thai Noodle Salad, 39–40
   Three-Pepper Chili, 140–141
   Tomato, Pepper, and Cilantro
     Soup, 77
   Vegetable Stir-Fry with Ginger
     Sauce, 132–133
   Warm Pasta Salad, 37
   Ziti Vegetable Salad, 52
Black beans, 10
   Burritos, Vegetarian, 138–139
   Couscous Casserole, Colorful,
     152–153
   Gingered Black Beans, 96
   Greens and Beans, Spicy, 90
   and Jicama Tostadas, 170
   One-Skillet Casserole, 150
   and Pasta Salad, Spicy, 30–31
   Pepper and Bean Enchiladas
     with Green Sauce, 160–161
   and Pepper Salad, 35
   Rice and Black Bean Salad, 48–49
   Salsa, 18–19
   Three-Pepper Chili, 140–141
   Vegetable Salad, 50
Black olives. *See* Olives
Bok choy. *See* Chinese cabbage
Bola peppers. *See* Jalapeo chiles
Broccoli
   Penne with, 125

Raw Vegetables with Soy-Ginger
    Sauce, 106
Thai Soup, 64–65
Vegetables in Raw Tomato
    Sauce, 176–177
Ziti Vegetable Salad, 52
Burritos
   Andrew's Mushroom
    Ta-Rito, 154
   Vegetarian, 138–139

C
Cabbage. *See also* Chinese cab-
    bage; Coleslaw
   Curried Apple Coleslaw, 43
   Soup, 67
   Sweet & Sour Cabbage, 179
   Sweet & Spicy Slaw, 34
   Vegetable Salad, 36
Calamata olives
   Chickpea and Pasta Salad,
    Spicy, 54–55
   Mediterranean Rice, 95
   Penne with, 113
   Peppers Stuffed with Pasta and
    Cheese, 120–121
   Vegetables in Raw Tomato
    Sauce, 176–177
   Warm Pasta Salad, 37
   Ziti Vegetable Salad, 52
Cannellini beans in Three-Pepper
    Chili, 140–141
Canola oil, 2
Capsicums. *See* Bell peppers
Carrots
   Black Bean
    One-Skillet Casserole, 150
    Vegetable Salad, 50
   and Cilantro Rice, 99
   Curried Apple Coleslaw, 43
   Curried Vegetables, 158–159
   Curried Vegetable Soup, 63
   Four-Alarm Stir-Fry, 168–169
   Fried Rice, Hot & Spicy, 155
   Jicama Slaw with Cilantro Vinai-
    grette, 47

Pepperpot Soup, 60–61
Raw Vegetables with Soy-Ginger
    Sauce, 106
Red Pepper Soup, 71
Saucy Carrots and Green
    Beans, 103
Sweet and Hot Carrots, 93
Thai Noodle Salad, 39–40
Tomato, Pepper, and Cilantro
    Soup, 77
Vegetable Broth, 58–59
Vegetable Salad, Spicy, 29
Vegetables in Raw Tomato
    Sauce, 176–177
Ziti Vegetable Salad, 52
Casseroles
    Black Bean One-Skillet Cas-
        serole, 150
    Couscous Casserole, Colorful,
        152–153
    Eggplant Casserole, Spicy, 167
    Fiery Zucchini Casserole, 148
    Vegetable-Pepper Casse-
        role, 149
Cauliflower, Curried Vegetables
    with, 158–159
Cayenne. See Bell peppers
Celery
    Black Bean and Pepper
        Salad, 35
    Curried Corn Soup, 66
    Curried Vegetable Soup, 63
    Lime-Curry Orzo, 111
    Pepperpot Soup, 60–61
    Potato-Jicama Salad, 44–45
    Red Pepper Soup, 71
    Shish Kabobs, Spicy, 142–143
    Vegetable Broth, 58–59
    Waldorf Salad, Curried, 32
Chayote squash in Quick Mexican
    Vegetables, 89
Cheddar cheese
    Andrew's Mushroom
        Ta-Rito, 154
    Black Bean One-Skillet Cas-
        serole, 150

Burritos, Vegetarian, 138–139
Chile and Sour Cream Quesadil-
    las, 134–135
Corn Chowder, Spicy, 72–73
Mexican "Quiche," 156–157
Pepper and Bean Enchiladas
    with Green Sauce, 160–161
and Tomato, and Hot Pepper
    Sandwiches, 166
Cheeses. See also specific
    cheeses
    Rice with Cheese, 92
    and Tomato, and Hot Pepper
        Sandwiches, 166
    Watercress, Gorgonzola, and
        Pear Salad, 40–41
    Zucchini-Basil Soup, 68–69
Cherry peppers. See Bell peppers
Cherry tomatoes
    Shish Kabobs, Spicy, 142–143
    Warm Pasta Salad, 37
Chervil, 3, 7
Chickpeas. See Garbanzo beans
Chilaca peppers, 8
Chile and Sour Cream Quesadillas,
    134–135
Chili, Three-Pepper, 140–141
Chili powder, 4
Chinese cabbage
    Greens and Beans, Spicy, 90
    Thai Soup, 64–65
Chives, 3, 7
    Cold, Spicy Cucumber Soup, 78
    Fettuccine with Peas and
        Peppers, 118
    Spaghetti Verdura, 119
    Vegetables in Raw Tomato
        Sauce, 176–177
Cilantro, 7
    Andrew's Mushroom
        Ta-Rito, 154
    Black Bean
        and Pepper Salad, 35
        Salsa, 19
    Carrot and Cilantro Rice, 99
    Mexican Vegetables, Quick, 89

Mushroom and Cilantro
Tostadas, 144–145
Pepperpot Soup, 60–61
Pineapple Salsa, 22
Pineapple Stir–Fried Rice, 178
Rice and Black Bean Salad,
48–49
Rice with Cheese, 92
Spicy Avocado Salsa, 20
Spicy Peach Salsa, 21
Thai Soup, 64–65
Tomato, Pepper, and Cilantro
Soup, 77
Coconut milk
Thai Noodle Salad, 39–40
Cold, Spicy Cucumber Soup, 78
Cold–press olive oil, 2
Cold Tomato and Roasted Pepper
Soup, 76
Coleslaw
Curried Apple Coleslaw, 43
Jicama Slaw with Cilantro Vin-
aigrette, 47
Sweet and Spicy Slaw, 34
Colorful Rice and Black Bean
Salad, 48–49
Corn
Black Bean Vegetable Salad, 50
Curried Corn Soup, 66
Spicy Corn Chowder, 72–73
Spicy Corn Salad, 53
Corn Chowder, Spicy, 72–73
Corn Salad, Spicy, 53
Couscous Casserole, Colorful,
152–153
Creamy Gazpacho, 75
Cubanelle peppers, 8
Cucumber
-Dill Dressing, 12
Cucumbers
Cold, Spicy Cucumber
Soup, 78
and Dill Salad, 51
Gazpacho, 75
Thai Cucumber Salad, 42
Vegetable Salad, 36
Vegetable Salad, Spicy, 29

Cumin
and Dill Dressing, 12–13
Curried Apple Coleslaw, 43
Curried Corn Soup, 66
Curried Fried Rice, 107
Curried Vegetables, 158–159
Curried Vegetable Soup, 63
Curried Waldorf Salad, 32
Curry powder, 4

D
De Arbol peppers. See Bell peppers
Dilled Zucchini Soup, 62
Dill weed, 7
Cold, Spicy Cucumber
Soup, 78
Cucumber and Dill Salad, 51
Cucumber-Dill Dressing, 12
Cumin and Dill Dressing, 12–13
Vegetable Salad, Spicy, 29
Zucchini Soup, Dilled, 62
Dressings, 8
Asparagus with Ginger–Lemon
Dressing, 83
Cucumber-Dill Dressing, 12
Cumin and Dill Dressing, 12–13
Ginger-Lemon Dressing, 83
Greek Dressing, 14–15
Honey Mustard Dressing, 17
Hot Vinegar, 14
jalapeo and Lime Dressing, 11
Rosemary Vinaigrette, 16
Wine Vinaigrette, 17

E
Eggplant
Grilled Vegetables with Ginger
Barbecue Sauce, 162–163
Sicilian Pizza, 123
Spicy Eggplant Casserole, 167
Eggs
Mexican "Quiche," 156–157
Mex-Italian Frittata, 151
Enchiladas
Pepper and Bean Enchiladas
with Green Sauce, 160–161
Spicy Enchilada Sauce, 24–25

Enchilada Sauce, Spicy, 24–25
Extra-virgin olive oil, 2

F
Feta cheese
   Lime-Curry Orzo, 111
   Mediterranean Rice, 95
   Penne with Calamata
     Olives, 113
Fettuccine
   Fresh Tomato Fettuccine, 128
   with Garlic and Zucchini, 117
   with Peas and Peppers, 118
Fiery Zucchini Casserole, 148
Food Front, 81
Four-Alarm Stir-Fry, 168–169
Fresh Tomato Fettuccine, 128
Fresno peppers. See Bell peppers
Fried Rice, Hot & Spicy, 155
Frittata, Mex-Italian, 151
Fritters, Simple and Spicy Zuc-
   chini, 97
Fruit Curry over Rice, 172–173

G
Garbanzo beans
   Bean Salad with Orange Vinai-
     grette, 56
   and Pasta Salad, Spicy, 54–55
   Snappy Garbanzos, 94
Garlic, 7
   Asian "Pesto" Pasta, 129
   Black Bean One–Skillet
     Casserole, 150
   Burritos, Vegetarian, 138–139
   Cabbage Soup, 67
   Curried Corn Soup, 66
   Curried Vegetables, 158–159
   Curried Vegetable Soup, 63
   Dilled Zucchini Soup, 62
   Eggplant Casserole, Spicy, 167
   Enchilada Sauce, Spicy, 24–25
   Fiery Zucchini Casserole, 148
   Fresh Tomato Fettuccine, 128
   Gazpacho, 75
   Green Beans, Spicy, 91
   Greens and Beans, Spicy, 90

Grilled Vegetables with Ginger
   Barbecue Sauce, 162–163
Gruyere Potatoes, 88
Hot Pesto, 24
Lemon Spaghetti, 112
Mediterranean Rice, 95
Penne with Broccoli, 125
Penne with Peppers, 116
Pepperpot Soup, 60–61
Pizza Sauce, 23
Shish Kabobs, Spicy, 142–143
Sicilian Pizza, 123
Sweet & Sour & Spicy, 136–137
Vegetable Broth, 58–59
Vegetable-Pepper Casse
   role, 149
Vegetable Stir-Fry with Ginger
   Sauce, 132–133
Zucchini-Basil Soup, 68–69
Zucchini Fritters, Simple and
   Spicy, 97
Zucchini Stuffed with Herbs and
   Cheese, 164–165
Gazpacho, 75
   Creamy Gazpacho, 75
Ginger, 84–85
   Asian "Pesto" Pasta, 129
   Asparagus with Ginger-Lemon
     Dressing, 83
   Black Beans, Gingered, 96
   Curried Fried Rice, 107
   Four-Alarm Stir-Fry, 168–169
   Fruit Curry over Rice, 172–173
   Greens and Beans, Spicy, 90
   Grilled Vegetables with Ginger
     Barbecue Sauce, 162–163
   Lime-Curry Orzo, 111
   Mushroom-Ginger Pasta, 122
   Pineapple-Curry Rice, 105
   Raw Vegetables with Soy–Ginger
     Sauce, 106
   Slaw, Sweet and Spicy, 34
   Sweet & Sour Cabbage, 179
   Teriyaki Mushrooms and
     Peppers, 100
   Thai Noodle Salad, 39–40
   Thai Soup, 64–65

Vegetable Salad, 36
Vegetable Stir-Fry with Ginger
    Sauce, 132–133
Gingered Black Beans, 96
Goat cheese, Peppers Stuffed with
    Pasta and, 120–121
Gorgonzola, Watercress, and Pear
    Salad, 40–41
Greek Dressing, 14–15
Green beans
    Curried Vegetables, 158–159
    Curried Vegetable Soup, 63
    in Hazelnut Butter, 103
    Quick Vegetable Stew, 70
    Salad, 46
    Saucy Carrots and Green
        Beans, 103
    Spanish Rice, Vegetables in,
        180–181
    Spicy Green Beans, 91
Green bell peppers. See Bell pep-
    pers
Green onions
    Carrot and Cilantro Rice, 99
    Mexican "Quiche," 156–157
Green Sauce, Mexican, 26
Greens and Beans, Spicy, 90
Grilled Vegetables with Ginger Bar-
    becue Sauce, 162–163
Gruyère Potatoes, 88
Guajillo peppers. See Bell peppers

H
Habanero chiles
    Black Bean and Pasta Salad,
        Spicy, 30–31
    Thai Soup, 64–65
Harissa, 18
Hazelnut Butter, Green Beans in,
    103
Herbs, 2–3. See also specific herbs
    chart on using, 7
Honey Mustard Dressing, 17
Hot chile peppers. See Bell peppers
Hot Pepper Sauce, Spaghetti
    with, 124
Hot Pesto, 24

Hot Vinegar, 14
Hungarian yellow wax peppers, 8

I
Italian peppers. See Bell peppers

J
Jack cheese
    Andrew's Mushroom
        Ta-Rito, 154
    Burritos, Vegetarian, 138–139
    Chile and Sour Cream Quesadil-
        las, 134–135
    Mexican "Quiche," 156–157
    Mex-Italian Frittata, 151
Jalapeño chiles, 8
    Andrew's Mushroom
        Ta-Rito, 154
    Baked Zucchini with Pepper
        Sauce, 174–175
    Black Bean Salsa, 19
    Black Bean Vegetable
        Salad, 50
    Burritos, Vegetarian, 138–139
    Chile and Sour Cream Quesadil-
        las, 134–135
    Cold Tomato and Roasted Pep-
        per Soup, 76
    Corn Salad, Spicy, 53
    Couscous Casserole, Colorful,
        152–153
    Enchilada Sauce, Spicy, 24–25
    Four-Alarm Stir-Fry, 168–169
    Fresh Tomato Fettuccine, 128
    Gazpacho, 75
    Gingered Black Beans, 96
    Green Beans, Spicy, 91
    Hot Pesto, 24
    and Lime Dressing, 11
    Mexican "Quiche," 156–157
    Mexican Stuffed Peppers,
        146–147
    Mex-Italian Frittata, 151
    Mushroom and Cilantro
        Tostadas, 144–145
    Pineapple Stir-Fried Rice, 178
    Quick Vegetable Stew, 70

Red Pepper Soup, 71
Rice
and Black Bean Salad, 48–49
with Cheese, 92
and Raisins, Hot, Spicy, 84–85
Spaghetti with Hot Pepper
Sauce, 124
Spanish Rice, 98
Spicy Peach Salsa, 21
Sweet & Sour & Spicy, 136–137
Thai Soup, 64–65
Jicama
Black Bean
and Jicama Tostadas, 170
Salsa, 19
Mexican Vegetables, Quick, 89
Potato-Jicama Salad, 44–45
Slaw with Cilantro Vinai-
grette, 47
Vegetable Salad, 36

K
Kalamata olives. *See* Calamata
olives
Kidney beans
Bean Salad with Orange Vinai-
grette, 56
Greens and Beans, Spicy, 90
Spanish Rice, Vegetables in, 180–181
Three-Pepper Chili, 140–141
Kosher salt, 4

L
Lemon Herb Rice, 101
Lemon Spaghetti, 112
Lettuce in Vegetable Broth, 58–59
Lime-Curry Orzo, 111

M
Marjoram, 3, 7
Mediterranean Rice, 95
Mexican Green Sauce, 26
Mexican "Quiche," 156–157
Mexican Stuffed Peppers, 146–147
Mexican Vegetables, Quick, 89
Mex-Italian Frittata, 151
Mint leaves, 7

Monterey jack cheese. *See* Jack
cheese
Mozzarella cheese
Peppers Stuffed with Pasta and
Cheese, 120–121
Sicilian Pizza, 123
Mushrooms
Andrew's Mushroom Ta-Rito, 154
Cabbage Soup, 67
and Cilantro Tostadas, 144–145
Fettuccine with Peas and
Peppers, 118
Four-Alarm Stir-Fry, 168–169
-Ginger Pasta, 122
Lemon Spaghetti, 112
Raw Vegetables with Soy-Ginger
Sauce, 106
Shish Kabobs, Spicy, 142–143
Spaghetti with Hot Pepper
Sauce, 124
Spinach Salad, Sweed, 33
Sweet & Sour & Spicy,
136–137
Teriyaki Mushrooms and
Peppers, 100
Thai Soup, 64–65
Vegetable Stir-Fry with Ginger
Sauce, 132–133
Zucchini Stuffed with Herbs and
Cheese, 164–165
Mustard
Grilled Vegetables with Ginger
Barbecue Sauce, 162–163
Honey Mustard Dressing, 17
Spaghetti Verdura, 119

N
New Mexican chiles, 8
Enchilada Sauce, Spicy, 24–25
Pepperpot Soup, 60–61
Tomato, Pepper, and Cilantro
Soup, 77
Niçoise olives
Vegetables in Raw Tomato
Sauce, 176–177
Warm Pasta Salad, 37
Noodles. *See* Pasta

O

Oils, 2
Olive oils, 2
Olives. *see also* Calamata olives;
  niçoise olives
  Potato-Jicama Salad, 44–45
  Sicilian Pizza, 123
  Ziti Vegetable Salad, 52
Onions
  Andrew's Mushroom Ta-Rito, 154
  Black Bean
    One-Skillet Casserole, 150
    and Pepper Salad, 35
  Burritos, Vegetarian, 138–139
  Cheese, Tomato, and Hot Pep-
    per Sandwiches, 166
  Chickpea and Pasta Salad,
    Spicy, 54–55
  Cold Tomato and Roasted Pep-
    per Soup, 76
  Corn Salad, Spicy, 53
  Curried Corn Soup, 66
  Curried Vegetables, 158–159
  Curried Vegetable Soup, 63
  Four-Alarm Stir-Fry, 168–169
  Fried Rice, Hot & Spicy, 155
  Gazpacho, 75
  Grilled Vegetables with Ginger
    Barbecue Sauce, 162–163
  Jicama Slaw with Cilantro Vinai-
    grette, 47
  Lime-Curry Orzo, 111
  Mexican Stuffed Peppers, 146–147
  Mexican Vegetables, Quick, 89
  Mushroom-Ginger Pasta, 122
  Penne with Broccoli, 125
  Pepperpot Soup, 60–61
  Pineapple Salsa, 22
  Pizza Sauce, 23
  Potato
    -Jicama Salad, 44–45
    Pancakes, Spicy, 102
  Quick Vegetable Stew, 70
  Ratatouille Pizza, 114–115
  Red Pepper Soup, 71
  Rice
    with Cheese, 92

  with Raisins, Hot, Spicy, 84–85
  Simple Summer Vegetables, 86
  Spanish Rice, 98
    Vegetables in, 180–181
  Spicy Peach Salsa, 21
  Sweet & Sour Cabbage, 179
  Sweet & Sour & Spicy, 136–137
  Tomato, Pepper, and Cilantro
    Soup, 77
  Vegetable Broth, 58–59
  Vegetable Salad, 36
    Spicy, 29
  Vegetable Stir-Fry with Ginger
    Sauce, 132–133
  Warm Pasta Salad, 37
  Zucchini–Basil Soup, 68–69
Oregano, 7
Orzo
  Lime-Curry Orzo, 111
  Peppers Stuffed with Pasta and
    Cheese, 120–121

P

Pancakes, Spicy Potato, 102
Parmesan cheese
  Fettuccine with Peas and
    Peppers, 118
  Lemon Spaghetti, 112
  Penne with Calamata
    Olives, 113
  Simple Summer Vege-
    tables, 86
  Vegetable-Pepper Casse-
    role, 149
  Zucchini
    -Basil Soup, 68–69
    Fritters, Simple and
      Spicy, 97
    Stuffed with Herbs and
      Cheese, 164–165
Parsley, 3, 7
  Peach Salsa, Spicy, 21
  Peppers Stuffed with Pasta and
    Cheese, 120–121
  Saucy Carrots and Green
    Beans, 103
  Tomatoes with Parsley, 87

Vegetable Broth, 58–59
Ziti with Herbs, 126–127
Pasilla peppers, 8
Pasta. *see also* Pasta salads
    Asian "Pesto" Pasta, 129
    Fettuccine
        Fresh Tomato Fettuccine, 128
        with Garlic and Zuc-
            chini, 117
        with Peas and Peppers, 118
    Hot Pepper Sauce, Spaghetti
        with, 124
    Lemon Spaghetti, 112
    Lime-Curry Orzo, 111
    Mushroom-Ginger Pasta, 122
    Penne
        with Broccoli, 125
        with Calamata Olives, 113
        with Peppers, 116
    Peppers Stuffed with Pasta and
        Cheese, 120–121
    Spaghetti
        with Hot Pepper Sauce, 124
        Lemon Spaghetti, 112
        Verdura, 119
    Ziti
        with Herbs, 126–127
        Vegetable Salad, 52
Pasta salads
    Black Bean and Pasta Salad,
        Spicy, 30–31
    Chickpea and Pasta Salad,
        Spicy, 54–55
    Thai Noodle Salad, 39–40
    Warm Pasta Salad, 37
    Ziti Vegetable Salad, 52
Peaches
    Fruit Curry over Rice, 172–173
    Spicy Peach Salsa, 21
Peanuts in Asian "Pesto"
    Pasta, 129
Pear, Watercress, and Gorgonzola
    Salad, 40–41
Peas
    Curried Fried Rice, 107
    Fettuccine with Peas and
        Peppers, 118

Spanish Rice, Vegetables in,
    180–181
Pecorino cheese Lemon
    Spaghetti, 112
Peeling, 4
Penne
    with Broccoli, 125
    with Calamata Olives, 113
    with Peppers, 116
Pepper and Bean Enchiladas with
    Green Sauce, 160–161
Pepperpot Soup, 60–61
Peppers, 3. *See also* specific pep-
        pers and chiles
    chart for using, 8
    roasting, 4
Pesto
    Asian "Pesto" Pasta, 129
    basil-cilantro pesto, 57
    Hot Pesto, 24
Pickles in Potato-Jicama Salad,
    44–45
Pineapple
    -Curry Rice, 105
    Fruit Curry over Rice, 172–173
    Salsa, 22
    Stir-Fried Rice with, 178
Pine nuts
    Hot Pesto, 24
    Penne with Broccoli, 125
    Peppers Stuffed with Pasta and
        Cheese, 120–121
Pistone, Bob, 81
Pizzas
    Ratatouille Pizza, 114–115
    Sauce for, 23
    Sicilian Pizza, 123
Plums in Fruit Curry over Rice,
    172–173
Poblano peppers, 8
Potatoes
    Cabbage Soup, 67
    Gruyere Potatoes, 88
    -Jicama Salad, 44–45
    Pancakes, Spicy Potato, 102
    Red Pepper Soup, 71
    and Rice with Spice, 171

Spanish Rice, Vegetables in,
180–181
Stir-Fried Red Potatoes, 82
Zucchini-Basil Soup, 68–69
Protein deficiency myth, 5

Q
Quesadillas, Chile and Sour
Cream, 134–135
Quiche, Mexican, 156–157
Quick Mexican Vegetables, 89
Quick Vegetable Stew, 70

R
Raisins
Curried Apple Coleslaw, 43
Rice and Raisins, Hot, Spicy,
84–85
Waldorf Salad, Curried, 32
Ratatouille Pizza, 114–115
Raw Vegetables with Soy–Ginger
Sauce, 106
Red bell peppers. See Bell peppers
Red Pepper Soup, 71
Red wine vinegar, 2
Rice
and Black Bean Salad, 48–49
Carrot and Cilantro Rice, 99
with Cheese, 92
Curried Fried Rice, 107
Curried Vegetables, 158–159
Fiery Zucchini Casserole, 148
Four-Alarm Stir-Fry, 168–169
Fried Rice, Hot & Spicy, 155
Fruit Curry over, 172–173
Lemon Herb Rice, 101
Mediterranean Rice, 95
Pepperpot Soup, 60–61
Pineapple-Curry Rice, 105
Potatoes and Rice with Spice, 171
and Raisins, Hot, Spicy, 84–85
Spanish Rice, 98
Vegetables in, 180–181
Sweet & Sour Cabbage, 179
Vegetable-Pepper Casse-
role, 149

Vegetable Stir-Fry with Ginger
Sauce, 132–133
Rice vinegar, 2
Ricotta cheese
Couscous Casserole, Colorful,
152–153
Penne with Peppers, 116
Roasting, 4
Rosemary, 7
Vinaigrette, 16

S
Sage, 7
Salad burnet, 3
Salad dressings. See Dressings
Salads, 27–54. See also Coleslaw;
Pasta salads
Bean Salad with Orange Vinai-
grette, 56
Black Bean
and Pasta Salad, Spicy,
30–31
and Pepper Salad, 35
Vegetable Salad, 50
Chickpea and Pasta Salad,
Spicy, 54–55
Corn Salad, Spicy, 53
Cucumber and Dill Salad, 51
Curried Apple Coleslaw, 43
Green Bean Salad, 46
Potato-Jicama Salad, 44–45
Rice and Black Bean Salad,
48–49
Spinach Salad, Sweet, 33
Sweet and Spicy Slaw, 34
Thai Cucumber Salad, 42
Thai Noodle Salad, 39–40
Vegetable Salad, 36
Spicy, 29
Waldorf Salad, Curried, 32
Watercress, Gorgonzola, and
Pear Salad, 40–41
Ziti Vegetable Salad, 52
Salsas, 9–10. See also Sauces
Avocado Salsa, Spciy, 20
Black Bean Salsa, 18–19

Mexican "Quiche," 156–157
Peach Salsa, Spicy, 21
Pineapple Salsa, 22
Sandwiches with Cheese, Tomato,
    and Hot Pepper, 166
Sauces, 10. See also Salsas
    Enchilada Sauce, Spicy, 24–25
    Harissa, 18
    Hot Pesto, 24
    Mexican Green Sauce, 26
    Pizza Sauce, 23
    Soy-Ginger Sauce, 106
Saucy Carrots and Green
    Beans, 103
Scallions
    Fettuccine with Peas and
        Peppers, 118
    Fried Rice, Hot & Spicy, 155
    Spaghetti Verdura, 119
    Vegetables in Raw Tomato
        Sauce, 176–177
Scotch bonnet chiles, 8
    Black Bean and Pasta Salad,
        Spicy, 30–31
    Thai Soup, 64–65
    Ziti with Herbs, 126–127
Serrano chiles
    Black Bean and Pepper
        Salad, 35
    Black Bean One–Skillet
        Casserole, 150
    Chile and Sour Cream Quesadil-
        las, 134–135
    Corn Chowder, Spicy, 72–73
    Couscous Casserole, Colorful,
        152–153
    Fresh Tomato Fettuccine, 128
    Sicilian Pizza, 123
    Slaw, Sweet and Spicy, 34
    Sweet & Sour & Spicy, 136–137
    Vegetable-Pepper Casserole, 149
Shish Kabobs, Spicy, 142–143
Sicilian Pizza, 123
Simple Summer Vegetables, 86
Slaw, Sweet & Spicy, 34
Snappy Garbanzos, 94

Snow peas in Thai Noodle Salad,
    39–40
Soups, 57–79
    Avocado Soup, 79
    Cabbage Soup, 67
    cold soups
        Spicy Cucumber Soup, 78
        Tomato and Roasted
            Pepper Soup, 76
    Corn Chowder, Spicy, 72–73
    Creamy Gazpacho, 75
    Curried Corn Soup, 66
    Curried Vegetable Soup, 63
    Dilled Zucchini Soup, 62
    Gazpacho, 75
    Pepperpot Soup, 60–61
    Red Pepper Soup, 71
    Thai Soup, 64–65
    Tomato
        Pepper, and Cilantro
            Soup, 77
        Soup, Spicy, 74
    Vegetable Broth, 58–59
    Zucchini-Basil Soup, 68–69
Sour cream
    Avocado Soup, 79
    Chile and Sour Cream Quesadil-
        las, 134–135
    Cucumber–Dill Dressing, 12
    Mushroom-Ginger Pasta, 122
Spaghetti
    with Hot Pepper Sauce, 124
    Lemon Spaghetti, 112
    Verdura, 119
Spanish Rice, 98
    Vegetables in, 180–181
Spices, 2–3
Spinach Salad, Sweet, 33
Stew, Quick Vegetable, 70
Stir-fry
    Four-Alarm Stir-Fry,
        168–169
    Pineapple Stir-Fried Rice, 178
    Red Potatoes, Stir–Fried, 82
    Vegetable Stir-Fry with Ginger
        Sauce, 132–133

Stuffed peppers
  Mexican Stuffed Peppers, 146–147
    with Pasta and Cheese, 120–121
Summer savory, 3, 7
Sunflower oil, 2
Sunflower seeds in Hot Pesto, 24
Sweet and Hot Carrots, 93
Sweet Banana peppers, 8
Sweet peppers. *See* Bell peppers
Sweet & Sour Cabbage, 179
Sweet & Sour & Spicy, 136–137
Sweet & Spicy Slaw, 34
Sweet Spinach Salad, 33

T
Tabasco, 8
Tarragon, 7
Teriyaki Mushrooms and Peppers, 100
Thai Cucumber Salad, 42
Thai Noodle Salad, 39–40
Thai Soup, 64–65
Three-Pepper Chili, 140–141
Thyme, 7
Tofu, 1
Tomatoes. *See also* Cherry tomatoes
  Andrew's Mushroom Ta-Rito, 154
  Black Bean Vegetable Salad, 50
  Cheese, Tomato, and Hot Pepper Sandwiches, 166
  Cold Tomato and Roasted Pepper Soup, 76
  Curried Vegetable Soup, 63
  Eggplant Casserole, Spicy, 167
  Fiery Zucchini Casserole, 148
  Fresh Tomato Fettuccine, 128
  Gazpacho, 75
  Green Beans, Spicy, 91
  Mediterranean Rice, 95
  Mexican "Quiche," 156–157
  Mexican Stuffed Peppers, 146–147
  with Parsley, 87

peeling/seeding, 4
  and Pepper and Cilantro Soup, 77
  Pepperpot Soup, 60–61
  Pizza Sauce, 23
  Quick Vegetable Stew, 70
  Rice with Cheese, 92
  Snappy Garbanzos, 94
  Soup, Spicy, 74
  Spanish Rice, Vegetables in, 180–181
  Spicy Avocado Salsa, 20
  Three-Pepper Chili, 140–141
  Vegetable-Pepper Casserole, 149
  Vegetable Salad, Spicy, 29
  Vegetables in Raw Tomato Sauce, 176–177
  Zucchini-Basil Soup, 68–69
Tomato juice
  Gazpacho, 75
  Snappy Garbanzos, 94
Tomato peppers, 8
Tortillas
  Andrew's Mushroom Ta-Rito, 154
  Black Bean and Jicama Tostadas, 170
  Burritos, Vegetarian, 138–139
  Chile and Sour Cream Quesadillas, 134–135
  Mexican "Quiche," 156–157
  Mushroom and Cilantro Tostadas, 144–145
  Pepper and Bean Enchiladas with Green Sauce, 160–161
Tostadas
  Black Bean and Jicama Tostadas, 170
  Mushroom and Cilantro Tostadas, 144–145
Turnips in Vegetable Broth, 58–59

V
Vegetables. *see also* specific vegetables
  Broth, 58–59

-Pepper Casserole, 149
in Raw Tomato Sauce, 176–177
in Spanish Rice, 180–181
Stir-Fry with Ginger Sauce,
132–133
Vegetable Salad, 36
Spicy, 29
Vegetarian Burritos, 138–139
Vinegars, 2
Hot Vinegar, 14
Vitamins, 6

W

Waldorf Salad, Curried, 32
Walnuts in Watercress, Gorgonzola,
and Pear Salad, 40–41
Warm Pasta Salad, 37
Water chestnuts
Couscous Casserole, Colorful,
152–153
Thai Noodle Salad, 39–40
Watercress, 3, 7
and Gorgonzola, and Pear
Salad, 40–41
White vinegar, 2
Wine Vinaigrette, 17

Y

Yellow squash in Quick Vegetable
Stew, 70
Yogurt, 4
Cold, Spicy Cucumber
Soup, 78
Mushroom-Ginger Pasta, 122
Penne with Peppers, 116
Vegetable Salad, Spicy, 29

Z

Ziti
with Herbs, 126–127
Vegetable Salad, 52
Zucchini
Baked Zucchini with Pepper
Sauce, 174–175
-Basil Soup, 68–69
Burritos, Vegetarian, 138–139
Curried Vegetables, 158–159
Dilled Zucchini Soup, 62
Fettuccine with Garlic and, 117
Fiery Zucchini Casserole, 148
Fritters, Simple and Spicy, 97
Grilled Vegetables with Ginger
Barbecue Sauce, 162–163
Lemon Spaghetti, 112
Mexican Vegetables, Quick, 89
Mex-Italian Frittata, 151
Penne with Peppers, 116
Quick Vegetable Stew, 70
Ratatouille Pizza, 114–115
Shish Kabobs, Spicy, 142–143
Simple Summer Vegetables, 86
Spaghetti Verdura, 119
Stuffed with Herbs and Cheese,
164–165
Sweet & Sour & Spicy,
136–137
Vegetable-Pepper Casse-
role, 149
Vegetables in Raw Tomato
Sauce, 176–177
Vegetable Stir-Fry with Ginger
Sauce, 132–133
Ziti Vegetable Salad, 52

International Conversion Chart

These are not exact equivalents: they have been slightly rounded to make measuring easier.

LIQUID MEASUREMENTS

American	Imperial	Metric	Australian
2 tablespoons (1 oz.)	1 fl. oz.	30 ml	1 tablespoon
1/4 cup (2 oz.)	2 fl. oz.	60 ml	2 tablespoons
1/3 cup (3 oz.)	3 fl. oz.	80 ml	1/4 cup
1/2 cup (4 oz.)	4 fl. oz.	125 ml	1/3 cup
2/3 cup (5 oz.)	5 fl. oz.	165 ml	1/2 cup
3/4 cup (6 oz.)	6 fl. oz.	185 ml	2/3 cup
1 cup (8 oz.)	8 fl. oz.	250 ml	3/4 cup

SPOON MEASUREMENTS

American	Metric
1/4 teaspoon	1 ml
1/2 teaspoon	2 ml
1 teaspoon	5 ml
1 tablespoon	15 ml

WEIGHTS

US/UK	Metric
1 oz.	30 grams (g)
2 oz.	60 g
4 oz. (1/4 lb)	125 g
5 oz. (1/3 lb)	155 g
6 oz.	185 g
7 oz.	220 g
8 oz. (1/2 lb)	250 g
10 oz.	315 g
12 oz. (3/4 lb)	375 g
14 oz.	440 g
16 oz. (1 lb)	500 g
2 lbs	1 kg

OVEN TEMPERATURES

Farenheit	Centigrade	Gas
250	120	1/2
300	150	2
325	160	3
350	180	4
375	190	5
400	200	6
450	230	8